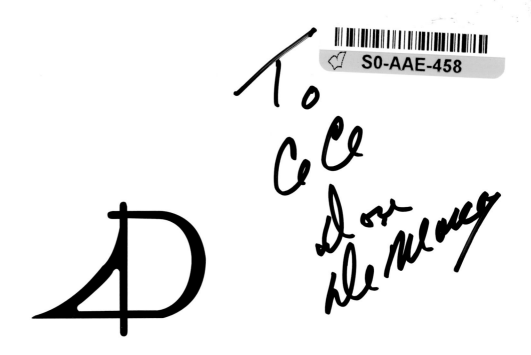

NANTUCKET

TASTE MEMORIES

The DeMarco Restaurant Cookbook

NANTUCKET
TASTE MEMORIES
The DeMarco Restaurant Cookbook

Text and Recipes:
Don DeMarco, Therese Collins, Dave DeMarco, Ann DeMarco, Dylan M. Bell

Photography:
Jeffrey Allen, Gary Brewster, Ann Rich, Natalie Hull Julia Naegele.
Book Cover Painting by Caroline Bucha, Vineyard painting by Brady Hansen

Graphics:
Justin Reynolds, Michael E. Wuerch

Published by DeMarco Restaurant Inc.
and Budrose Associates
240 East 79th St. Suite 2A
New York, New York 10021

ISBN 978-1-60402-757-0

Copyright © 2007 by Donald E. DeMarco

Printed in the United States of America
Robert L. Freudenheim/United Graphics/Buffalo, NY

DEDICATION

To my wife Therese and my
family and friends, with whom
I love, laugh, and eat well.

I had one wish. In the fairy tale the genie gave three wishes, I complained until I got mine.

CONTENTS

INTRODUCTION

Restaurants evolve like people; they are made of dreams, ambitions, goals, and flaws. A restaurant founder nurtures an idea into a business. There are good restaurants and good businesses; to have both takes hard work and a little luck. The key to all human enterprises is inspiration, and it should show up in every aspect of the business. The building, décor, and personnel create an environment derived from that inspiration and flow through to the food and wine. The result is truly a fine dining experience. The body of work herein is the story of one restaurant that could apply to many successful restaurants and businesses driven by the human spirit.

The nights spent dining with friends at my table in Nantucket, looking out onto the lantern lit cobblestones of India Street, are woven into a tapestry of treasured memories and images of the past twenty-seven years.

Thank you.

Don DeMarco, April 2007.

THE FOOD
FOOD'S PERSONAL MEANING

"We sit and say and dream
Among the rows of summer grass
No sounds abound
We taste our time"

DeM

Forget all that stuff you've heard about "you can't go home again"; you can do it through food. When dining, family memories are always present. As an adult, there is a memory of childhood every time you sit down to eat with family, friends or alone. It is always there. In a rapidly changing world, food and its meaning do not change. Your mother and/or your grandmother was the chef and the waitress; your father, brothers, sisters, aunts, uncles, cousins and friends were all your dining partners and helpers. The food provided the foundation for the continuum and convergence of their love. Dinner and stimulating talk among family members at the end of the day unraveled the world of toil and worry. And it was every day!

Modern life often intrudes on the family's evening meal. If this tradition is lost, much more will be at stake than just the taste of good food.

The table has long been the place of family comfort, wisdom, and at times, abundance. One has only to think of the phrases with the word table in them, which derive from an intimate interaction with family, friends, acquaintances and business colleagues. And how prominent the table is in our culture: family table, table talk, on-the-table, off-the-table, table hop, tabled, this side of the table, that side of the table, table wine, and table etiquette to name just a few.

OUR TABLE
THE ANNIVERSARY DINNER

A guest at the table
A young boy chosen to bear witness,
Too young to understand
But nods he in his entrance
Begin his sweet beginnings
That might pass down these anniversary gifts
Time present to time future to enrich so young
Who will celebrate his day
Imagined now, light-years away.

DeM

The restaurant table is perceived frequently as a personal place. Memories exist at certain tables like vaults where precious times have been stored, special places that customers have frequented throughout the years. People often remember exactly where they were seated when recalling their engagement, a birthday celebration, or an anniversary. They will request to be seated at the exact same table, which exists as a "spot" of memory — personal, private and permanent.

People have a way of opening up at their table in restaurants. Perhaps this is due to the familial setting and a sip of wine that triggers the sharing of intimate details of their lives, laying the foundation for life long friendships..

Dining alone is another matter. Most people strongly resist having dinner alone. They eat at a bar, at the counter of a diner, or order in and eat in front of a television set to minimize the stark realization of loneliness. Meals are meant to be shared. This is why many solitary diners choose to read. When we read, we no longer feel quite so alone.

COMFORT FOOD

THE FAMILY IS ALL THERE IS; ITS HISTORY AND ETERNAL CONSEQUENCES.

The concept of "comfort food" derives its meaning from the family meals of childhood, which continue to provide a taste of the past whenever it is consumed. Taste memories and table time are always present. American food in all working-class households was high in calories, carbohydrates, fat-laden, and delicious. Will Durant, the ancient history scholar, wrote "No civilization has progressed without stimulants." At the time, he was referring to alcohol and tobacco. Today, I would include food in that observation; meatloaf, mashed potatoes, fried chicken, macaroni and cheese, beef stew and grilled cheese sandwiches, etc., were part and parcel of everyone's comfort food menu. Unfortunately, it is seldom found properly prepared in restaurants or diners. What's missing is the "home-cooked" care and flavor, inherent in the atmosphere of the family table. If comfort food had a human face, whom would it look like?

The pleasure factor of food comes from its loving preparation, and its consumption ; it is a journey of complex delight. As the poet Kahlil Gabran said, "If you bake bread with indifference, you feed but half of man's hunger." Of course, restaurants have a lot to do with satisfaction and little to do with hunger, unless you eat in certain fancy establishments and go away slightly famished.

People need to express themselves; that doesn't mean you have to make things. One form of expression is in the public arena of a restaurant. The food you eat, the wine you drink, the ambiance you choose, the individuals with whom you dine, and those who serve you comprise your experience. Family recipes and style are a precious heritage, like real property in a personal estate. That heritage is the permanent architecture from your childhood memories which along with the gifts of the earth, guide you towards your future.

In a world of unsettling change, foods remain the same. What we do with food in restaurants or at home changes constantly. The potatoes in Van Gogh's haunting painting, The Potato Eaters, would taste the same today. In some fine contemporary Parisian restaurants the mashed potato has become a featured item.

Given the vast array of food items to choose from, the good cook always knows what goes together best. There is a saying, "what grows together, goes together." That which grew together in a specific climate and area, when combined usually tastes good.

When a cook today makes a recipe that has ancient roots, a light turns on in the creative process. The outcome has a world of subtle and infinite possibilities; no matter how many times you have made it before, it is as if it were the first time. Food and wine transforms us into lighter beings.

Food relieves the burden of the unknown and offers an oasis of goodness every time you sit with people you care about. The conversation and the experience elevates. Of course, the food has to be good, and you really do have to like the people.

Remember to cook more than is needed! History is replete with hunger. Savor abundance and waste nothing. Think of leftovers in the refrigerator as "little hugs waiting to happen," as my little niece once declared. At DeMarco, we are serving a third generation of patrons. They represent a true reflection of family etched in my memory as they come to dine as couples or in groups. Observing this transgenerational phenomenon is a perfect reaffirmation of family life being handed down, generation after generation, splendid and assured.

The sense of taste, developed over millions of years of evolution, is perhaps the most complex of the five senses. Taste and smell both are deeply entwined with that most elusive and fascinating of cerebral traits--memory. A whiff of saffron transports us to a sun-baked morning in a Mediterranean market; a few drops of wine deliver us to a late afternoon in a favorite vineyard.

With respect to taste, we sometimes exaggerate. How often do we hear the words, "That was the best I have ever tasted!" Such a statement may be true on rare occasions, but how would it stand up to a blind taste test? Feel free to accumulate those wondrous time bytes. To enjoy an experience without qualifying it as the "best ever" is liberating. Let your memory do the walking.

Texture, it is no accident that the preferred size of diced foods fits in the bed of human molars. Not only is there a smooth and sensual taste in the mouth, there is texture, often described by food writers as "mouth feel." Texture is often lost in modern cooking, probably due to the public's preference for food that is a little overcooked .

Even the sound of food being eaten reverberates through the ear and the cranium, creating still another sensation. Few eating pleasures can compare to the experience of the crunch, feel, and sound from fried chicken, potato chips, apples, crusty bread, peanuts and so on. Think about the first bite of a peanut: the initial crunch slowly mellows into its roasted flavor, lingering and provoking the wish for more.

Jeffrey Allen

The basic ingredients that go into our favorites are simple. When you taste something good, your palette expands and escalates into something extraordinary. The first sensation is striking and exciting, the second is delayed and subtle, and the third is slow and lingering. We should have a better word for what happens when something delicious hits the taste buds. The list of foods and wines that do this is long, but here are a few of the memorable ones: fresh baked bread and butter, roast glazed duck, dark chocolate, vanilla ice cream, and ripe watermelon.

Layers of Flavor: While the mind can clearly differentiate layers of taste and commit it to memory, the palette does it differently. The palette is a complex blending of taste sensations, separate and apart, as any experienced wine taster is aware. After the initial taste has receded, the next taste leads and quietly finishes the experience.

Regional Cooking: There is no mystery in regional cooking, but there is the knowledge to use the regions seasonal, available ingredients (preferably those grown, raised or fished in the immediate area). The New England boiled dinner and chowders is a good example of local culinary invention. Its distant Mediterranean counterpart, bouillabaisse, was originally a peasant dish composed of fish scraps, liberally laced with the saffron that grew wild in the south of France. Today, saffron sells for $300 per ounce. Regional dishes in any culture were not dictated by choice, but rather by poverty and what was readily available. Nature has an infinite capacity to produce a great quantity of foods within a micro geographical area, which explains the incalculable varieties of food in the world.

Beyond taste and smell, food is a visual experience. The sight of a pot of red sauce with sausage and meatballs, or a 3-inch-thick Porter House steak, or a steamed lobster and corn, is a visual pleasure driven by color and form. These foods are a product of the inventive ways everyday cooks have found to prepare and present foods throughout history.

The presentation of Italian food needs little enhancement. Salads and pastas enjoy the vivid colors naturally present and need little embellishment. Food, in its simplicity, is important; the natural look contributes to presentation. A recipe overwhelmed by too many ingredients and fanciful garnishes is an attempt to create illusions about food, which may on special occasions be appropriate.

The culinary art offers still another journey of the eye: its transformation of food from a raw, natural state into a cooked, fully prepared dish. In East of Eden, John Steinbeck rather graphically describes frying eggs: "...[he] broke the eggs and they jumped and flooded their edges to brown lace and made clucking sounds." In the old black skillet at home, the whites frayed at their bubbly borders, like worn, perforated lace curtains. The appetite, enhanced by the visual experience, is itself transformed, giving way to the anticipation of taste, making the pleasure of food a multi-sensory experience!

Nothing conjures up a multitude of memories like the aroma and taste of food. A moment of reflection will tell you how taste is affected by our memory of eating certain foods in the past and looking forward to the pleasure of eating the same food in the future an infinite number of times. Memory and taste, when combined, represent a unique experience for every individual; it is the one event, a common bond we all share that transports us from the past to the present at the speed of light.

The intimate connection between meal and memory was amply demonstrated some time ago, when I was out having dinner alone at an upscale restaurant. I had ordered my meal and was eagerly anticipating its arrival. Next to me, two young women were speaking loud enough for me to overhear their conversation. They were obviously having a great time, enjoying the evening and chatting amiably.

When they picked up their dinner menus to look over the selections, one of the women said to her friend: "Do you know what good food is?" I thought to myself, "Yes, I do," but I was not prepared for what I was about to hear. "Tomato soup and grilled cheese sandwich," she declared. Stopped dead in my tracks, I was no longer interested in the soon-to-appear veal chop or anything else except my neighbor's pronouncement. Why shun an elegant veal chop for a hot bowl of tomato soup and grilled cheese sandwich? This reason goes back to the original meaning of "comfort food". We are conditioned to order food that takes us back to our familiar "comfort" zone of the past—the "safety net" of our soul.

Some people may find it difficult to understand why we who love food and wine make such a fuss over it. We have no choice, our cultural heritage is bred in the bone.

LAYERED LEGENDS

Every culture has its own comfort foods. Among the most popular and universal are those that are stuffed or layered. Foods stuffed, wrapped, rolled and sandwiched, probably came about as a way to transport a meal or preserve it. The construct of lasagna, which actually means "layered" in Italian, is a prime example of this. In some form, it is a mainstay produced in virtually every culture.

The medieval diet of Britain included a pasta dish resembling lasagna, called loseyns. This dish required layers of flat sheets of pasta, separated by a cheese sauce. Its similarity to lasagna in its present-day form is obvious.

Historians studying medieval Italy produced documentation revealing that prior to 1390, the cookbook (libro di cucina) actually did contain the first known recipe for lasagna. The premise that lasagna is an Italian dish created a national "ownership" argument. Throughout history, however, the original birthplace of this dish has been disputed. Today, everybody makes a version of lasagna, and they are all good.

There are other delicious dishes similar to lasagna that layered or stuffed in some kind of bread, or covered with pastry crust, such as in chicken pot pie.

FOOD VARIATIONS

People love variety but no one wants their favorite dish to change every time they sit down to eat it. This is especially true of the food we grew up with and the dishes we order in favorite restaurants. A 500-year-old recipe can be duplicated using the same ingredients and techniques to this very day, but even the slightest change can provoke great displeasure at home or at a restaurant, even though the recipe may have been improved.

Food and wine have exerted a subtle force in all of civilization. Its reach touches religion, culture, politics and war. The everyday sustenance that made the good times wonderful and the bad times tolerable.

When immigrants settled in other nations of the world, they brought their recipes with them, dramatically influencing the host country's palette. From that palette emerged the modern art form of dining.

Italian cuisine came to America during the immigration from southern Italy where poverty was rampant, in circumstances similar to the Irish migration to America during the potato famine. The Italian cuisine brought to America was categorized as a hearty, spicy red sauce cuisine. The northern Italian influence in the United States didn't flourish until the 1970's. Today the cuisine of northern Italy is as popular as the traditional southern. Both are rich and complex—and strikingly different from each other in their variations. The art form of dining, practiced in the past mainly by the elite, is now enjoyed by many in today's world. It often exists in an informal personal setting like Sunday dinner. In the home where I grew up, a dozen people or more on weekends and holidays was the norm.

Modern fine dining changed the simplicity of the Old World cookery to the current wondrous cuisine, all too often leading to pretension and overpricing. Restaurants became theaters. To be seen in a fancy restaurant became a sign of prestige, involving the "proper," strategically placed table, a territorial imperative. The moment food is taken from the private to the public marketplace, it often suffers in the translation.

There have always been places in history where people could eat away from home. Only recently, probably following WWII when enough food could get to enough people, did the newly established American middle class venture out to restaurants in large numbers. At the time, the real treat was the act of going out to dinner; the food was secondary. The American appreciation of good food combined with an increasingly refined taste also started after WWII. This was the result of economic prosperity, travel to Europe, and the increased sophistication and diversity of American restaurants. The evolution continues today—nowhere more evident than in the proliferation of fusion cuisine--due to our-expanding global experience. The reliability and growing faith in the future began to erase the fear of our parents' and grandparents' generations, one step removed from the scarcity and hunger of their native countries and the Great American Depression.

Dinner was a moment of relief on a sweltering summer day or a frigid winter night. These moments, built around the solid structure of working families, provided the foundation for the great American middle class; the first ever in all of civilization.

FOOD AND ART

There exists in nature an important relationship between food and art. Aristotle's Golden Mean describes forms that appear in nature and are reproduced by man. We are compelled to do so because these forms are most pleasing to the eye. Human perception is drawn toward these proportions in all aspects of life. In the Golden Mean, there exists about a 2:3 or 1:618 ratio, whether the composition is constructed by straight or curved lines, shown in the diagrams on the next page. From the presentation of food to physics (the curved path of subatomic particles) to Da Vinci's paintings of clouds — all represent examples of the Golden Mean.

Examples of the Golden Mean in food are the rectangular form of many entrees presented in the middle of a dinner plate, the conical shapes of shellfish, or the popular crescent form of many pastries. All reflect a perfect fusion of food and art.

There are times when the overwhelming desire for taste and design can be carried too far. Food, unfortunately, is not immune to fads — not just what purports to be the "in" dishes (think Kobe hamburgers saddled with foie gras), conceived by overly ambitious chefs who catered them. Some of these precious constructions were such that the diner would hesitate to apply "bold knife and fork", as stated by MFK Fisher, to a meal for fear of destroying its beauty. It was as if the meal itself was not meant to be consumed but only to be admired.

FOOD AND THOUGHT

The language used to describe food instantly creates a cascade of images and sensations in the mind. Words elicit the dish, its flavor, even the melodious sound of its name.

A menu will list a dish such as Roast Chicken with Rosemary. The two main words "chicken" and "rosemary" have equal weight; their intended effect is the same. In reality, the flavor of the rosemary is lost, and not really worth mentioning because it is overpowered by the flavor of chicken. While such an image can be misleading, your taste buds do not lie. On the other hand, a dish like almond-crusted halibut actually conveys the taste of all its elements. The point here is to think of food as it is and do not be misled by a description.

COOKING: GETS A BAD NAME

The sheer drudgery involved in gathering, preparation, and cooking on an open fire throughout civilization had given cooking a bad name. Originally dictated by survival, prior to the food revolution in America (circa 1970), women growing up during the feminist movement viewed "slaving over a hot stove" as a burden, one that their mothers were duty-bound to do--a monotonous chore to be performed seven days a week.

This perception of cooking was so engrained that few intellectual, sophisticated woman of that era learned to enjoy cooking. Young women, instead of admiring their mother's culinary knowledge, abandoned it to restaurant chefs, cooking shows and food magazines.

Their daughters, who had no opportunity to learn how to cook at their mother's or grandmother's knee, became what Barbara Gibbs Ostmann and Jane L. Baker called "the lost generation" in The Recipe Writer's Handbook. They noted that "a staggering 45% of the respondents in a national food literacy survey, didn't know how many teaspoons are in a tablespoon." Nevertheless, some women, lucky enough to have come closer to the culinary arts than making reservations, soon discovered that the techniques observed through the media were those they had witnessed for years in their own homes, watching their mothers.

Career women, juggling near-impossible schedules, sought to reinstate the art of cooking into their lives by using prepared foods, a trend picked up by Los Angeles chef, Nancy Silverton, in her cookbook, A Twist of the Wrist: Quick Flavorful Meals with Ingredients From Jars, Cans, Bags and Boxes (Knopf). In an article published in the New York Times (April 8, 2007), she is quoted as saying: "The way people are eating at home, they are not cooking, not preparing, not even dumping out of a container!" Her latest effort is dedicated to luring them back into the proximity of the kitchen stove by using ingredients found on supermarket shelves—such as olive-oil packed tuna, beans, and tapenade. Overwhelming agendas still demand tasty food, albeit in non-labor-intensive recipes.

Perhaps by now we may have had enough of television cooks showing us how to use a pepper grinder, chop an onion, or operate a food processor. There is even a concept afloat that could be called "semi-made". Just what is that?—a meal made by a "semi-cook?" By narrating every detail, cooking shows have become momentary entertainment, a miraculous trick of perception which turns narration into entertainment. While cooking is a relaxing form of activity for some, it is not just simply that. It is an orderly creative process, one that everyone is capable of doing.

Cooking, like other crafts, involves multiple steps: from planning, presentation and table setting. Everyone has creative gifts in one form or another: painters, writers, photographers, pastry chefs, and architects, all express themselves in their own ways. The challenge is for a person to find a medium that corresponds to their talent.

There are a few rules to abide by when creating a meal. Keep it simple; concentrate on five main ingredients or less. The best way to control what you eat for good taste and good health is to cook it yourself. At a restaurant, be sure that the chef will accommodate your desires regarding fat and salt content, while preparing it the way you like.

Meat, fowl, fish and vegetables are foods whose natural state require little embellishment. Other foods like pasta, bread, and sauces are vehicles upon which other foods and flavors ride. Potato chips are a platform for fat and salt. For that matter, it is also misleading to hear media cooks talk about the juice from meat; it is not juice, it is just fat, fat, and more fat! The uniform line and porous nature of pasta and rice absorbs tasty sauces and delivers their flavors evenly in every bite. The absorbent quality of pasta and rice lends itself to savory sauces. The same principle of absorption is applied to the long, slow cooking of meats (cassoulet), where tastes become concentrated, intense and dramatic. People love the essence of a thing; it is what drives their desire to taste it thorough out their entire life. In a professional kitchen, twenty quarts of ingredients simmered for twenty four hours will yield four quarts of concentrated taste in the stock. A honey bee will make two million trips from flower to hive to produce one quart of honey.

Jeffrey Allen

PEASANT FOOD: FROM PAUPER TO PRINCE

Essentially, the food didn't change, but the way we thought about it did. A friend told me recently that when his parents were young, living in clustered housing, they would pull down the shades when they ate polenta, ashamed of eating what was then deemed to be "peasant" food. Nowadays, however, the stigma of polentas past has gone from "peasantry" to princely. Fancy restaurants celebrate not only these humble beginnings, but other equally less lofty basics, such as rice, beans, etc., (give or take a truffle or two).

Our knowledge of food, drink and the aesthetics of dining are derived mainly from the inventiveness of ordinary people who made a potato taste better and who grew a wild flower outside their hovel. They found ways to make inexpensive food items taste good.

Traditionally, as everyone knows, pasta is cooked in water and salt, the proven method for centuries. The pasta water is, of course, discarded. In most restaurants, after being drained from the boiling water, most pastas are finished in a sauté pan (approximately one minute) with the sauce specified on the menu. Everyone agrees that this method does produce the best-tasting pastas. Rice, too, can be cooked in a bouillon, producing a similar result.

For special occasions, however, boiling the pasta in a prepared sauce, either a tomato, vegetable or meat-flavored broth with all of the accompanying seasonings, produces a unique dish with a much deeper taste. This method infuses the sauce's flavor into the pasta for the entire boiling process (ten or fifteen minutes, as opposed to one minute in the sauté pan). If the sauce becomes too thick, it can always be diluted with water. My grandfather called this method of cooking "rich man's pasta."

Salt and bread was once consumed as a meal unto itself. Something as simple as salt was once the compensation paid to indentured miners in South Africa; it was equivalent to gold, transported, traded, and sold along the Salt Road of West Africa. Peasants were poor only in material assets, but their contribution to society, whether culinary or other artisan crafted products show their great spirit. Their lives, however impoverished, were also informed by talent, inspiration, grace and imbued by beauty, however rare--assets that are not defined by material wealth.

Peasants worked the land, grew their crops, and produced the goods, the lion's share of which was relinquished to the landlords. The history of war and the struggle for power and wealth have shown us that the underlying component always has been land. It comes as no surprise that women, in particular, were burdened very heavily during these conflicts and troubled periods in history, confined mostly to doing household chores: cooking, food-gathering, and other laborious tasks. Over the years, the feudal farm system under which they worked gave way to a hard-won freedom. As a result, peasants enjoyed a better meal at the end of the day. Their inventiveness, however, was constantly challenged by poverty..

Garlic, a common ingredient in many immigrant dishes, was often considered anathema because of its association with "foreigners". Now the stigma is all but forgotten. Once dubbed the "stinking rose," today garlic is a staple on nearly everyone's shell, not only for its taste, but also for its perceived health benefits. Now it is celebrated in dedicated festivals (think Gilroy) and sold in pill form in every corner health-food store or in drugstore chains alongside the vitamin capsules.

Today, even though they can afford better, people frequently prefer unpretentious food. Indeed, nobody would have perfected the art of sausage-making had there existed fine fresh filets of refrigerated beef. Simple "salt-of-the-earth" produce became the basis of what we now refer to as the "family meal"; good, solid, hearty food put together and served after a hard day's work. We had it every night in my childhood home and, as an adult, I still enjoy the "family meal" every summer night with the staff around the picnic table on the patio at DeMarco Restaurant.

Natalie Hull

FREEDOM OF CHOICE

**"THERE IS THE BEST SEASON IN THE GROUND
THAT WE HAVE HAD IN TWENTY YEARS."
-DIARY OF JESS BARNES, TEXAS FARMER**
JANUARY 28, 1931

- 25 -

The founding of America created a life for the masses once only dreamed about in all of history. The world waited for America to be born! Then witnessed the full measure of human talent unleashed in only 200years. Freedom of choice, life and liberty created other freedoms, such as personal tastes. Abundant food supply and a variety of choices for the multitudes were manifest during the great prosperity following WWII. In the final analysis, it is the inventiveness and ambition of ordinary citizens, working in an enterprise, which drives the great American socio-economic system forward. The beneficiaries of this history were born then -- the baby-boomers -- sandwiched as they were between WWII and the gold rush of technology, enabling them to experience opportunities beyond all imagining. This gift, which so many Americans enjoy today, stands in stark contrast to a past history of brutal oppression. And the new challenges of the millennium are on the global horizon to test us again.

The title of a popular novel Bonfire of the Vanities was taken from the era of Fra Girolamo Savonarola (1452-1498). This highly influential Catholic monk created the sumptuary laws in Florence, Italy, where people were imprisoned and tortured for the sinful pleasures of vanity. He sought to reform the people's entire way of life, and that included eating habits. (Ravioli with butter, for instance, was an indulgence.) Eventually imprisoned for his reactionary politics, he stood as a perfect example against all things a good appetite desires.

An abundant choice of food, however, does come with its problems. Getting enough protein into hard-working people has been an historic struggle. Ironically, today getting protein out of people in our culture has become a modern health crisis. Nature and physical work reduce stress, however today food and beverages are used as stress reducers, creating serious health risks. The American diet versus the Mediterranean diet is a good example. The sedentary life of most Americans, coupled with the modern diet, work against us: We cannot work off nearly enough of the rich foods and sugars we consume and, as a result, diabetes and obesity have become epidemic. Smartly, restaurants are cooking in olive oil instead of butter, the increased public health awareness has recently seen fast food establishments eliminating transfats. One seldom will see an obese farmer who works the land for a living.

Food cannot be seen alone but rather as part of an intergrated and balanced lifestyle, a source of good health, energy, and pleasure. Short-term hunger may serve a good purpose; missing a meal reminds us of our true nature, one of a constant state of vulnerability.

DON'T BE AFRAID

"A JUG OF WINE, A LOAF OF BREAD—AND THOU."
OMAR KHAYYÁM
THE RUBÁIYÁT

Omar Khayyám conjures up a trio of such great simplicity -- nothing in literary enterprise could be more perfect -- yet these seemingly "simple" things can be difficult to come by. Wine, bread, and "thou" never quite reach perfection. The simplest recipes are often the most difficult to execute. Consider two fried eggs and how often you have eaten them. Once in a while they are almost perfect; often just okay, and sometimes, inedible.

While the food revolution of the past twenty-five years in America has spawned a huge population of new cooks, my guess is that more than half of the general population still stays out of the kitchen. I've often wondered why. Almost everyone likes to eat and drink; it stands to reason, then, that almost everyone should

enjoy some cooking. The problem with cooking may well be the simple fear of making a mistake that everyone will know about. Food is so personal that a fear of cooking something that turns out badly may be a deterrent to giving it a try at all. As I write this, I am amused about some of my friends who hate cooking-- powerful CEOs, masters of the board room, intimidated by a kitchen.

Don't be intimidated; you have history behind you. Trust and be confident that someone, in your past, once made a living with their hands, the same hands that cared for babies, built machines and drove fast cars. Improvise and create, and you will discover a very telling moment.

Food is the most complete of all human experiences because it permeates all of life--from the gala birthday party to the last meal of the condemned.

You are already an expert; anyone who eats and drinks with joy and appreciation knows his or her own taste. Go with that knowledge.

People do not go to restaurants just for better food, they go out for a social function — to see and be seen—and to experience a variety of cuisines; not necessarily better, just different. It has been said that we go to restaurants to have salt and sugar put in our food.

Elevated temperatures of professional stoves result in the quick caramelization that everyone craves. Pleasing to the eye, the ubiquitous term "golden brown" is on every television cook's tongue; that coveted caramelization relies on high temperatures and high fat content, not always the healthiest method of cooking, depending on how often it is consumed. European food is great, but remember it is intensely seasoned with a very high fat content; that, plus the fact that you are having a wonderful, relaxing holiday, vastly increases the pure pleasure of eating.

It is also important not to listen to other peoples' notions about the proper preparation of food-- for example, how to dress pasta. When cooks say to use just enough to slightly coat the pasta, this is nonsense! If you love a certain sauce, why would you want less of it? People enjoy a lot of sauce. The idea of scarcity comes from poverty, hardly appropriate in a time of plenty! If it really is just about pasta, then try eating it plain.

Jeffrey Allen

WINE

There must be at least 10,000 books written about wine. For all of wine's complexity, there are a few fundamentals to keep in mind. Of all that I have read, anecdotes I have heard, and tastings I've attended, a simple story about a young man starting out in the wine business left the greatest impression on me. He was visiting a small vineyard in Italy, the winemaker took the time to point out the delicate intricacies of the two wines they were tasting. The first wine had been made from grapes grown on one side of a small stone wall, the second from grapes cultivated on the other side. Both were exceptionally good wines, but there was a remarkable difference in the tastes.

Common knowledge has it that wine is a highly nuanced beverage, affected by the slightest variations of climate, sun, shade and soil. Expert wine tasters pride themselves on not only determining which wine is in their glass, but also the year, and even the plot of ground on which the grapes were grown..

Recently confronted by the likes of Harold McGee and Daniel Patterson, who beg to differ in no uncertain terms. In an article entitled "Talk Dirt to Me" published in The New York Times Style Magazine (May 6, 2007), the authors debate the very popular assertion that you can taste the terrain in the wine. Describing the theory as an "appealing" one, and "a welcome link to nature and place in a de-localized world," there is only one problem, they declare: it's not true.

They contend that the inert materials absorbed by the grapevine growing in the earth uses sunlight to transform them into "sugars, acids, aromas, tannins, pigments and dozens of other molecules that make grapes and wine delicious." They go on to point out that the delicious flavors in question are really mostly the result of the interaction between the grapes and the yeast. Other unlikely-sounding components in the taste test are vine type, orientation, spacing, pruning, canopy management, irrigation and fertilizers. While where the grapes are grown does affect the taste of the wine, it does so indirectly, through the manipulations of the wine grower and the winemaker, as well as the chemistry between microbe and grape. "We don't taste a place in the wine. We taste a wine from a place," they conclude.

Such are the passions inspired by people who love wine, from the romantic to the scholarly, all make their contribution to the ancient culture of wine.

Wine evokes dramatic behavior in some people. At a tasting a few years ago, I overheard a wine salesman say while holding his glass, "This wine flirts with you." A woman responded wistfully, "Yes, but it's such a profound flirting!"

There are a few simple things to remember about wine:

1. Wine tends to fall into two categories, good and bad, not always dictated by price. You have to be in the right mood to drink a big wine. Wine may change your mood, but the fine ones require your cooperation. You must have the time to savor and appreciate; great wines are not meant to be gulped down. The food should complement the wine, and vice versa, although nowadays the conventional "rules" about what goes with what are often ignored without prejudice.

2. In a wine shop or while reading a wine list, stick with what you know. When you feel comfortable with your favorites, then it's time to experiment a bit. Find the three or four reds and whites you like (grape type) and learn to appreciate the different tastes produced by the multitude of winemakers of that particular grape. For example, there are hundreds of chardonnay wines produced in California alone, so don't be intimidated.

3. Trust your personal taste for wine, just as you would for food.

4. At home, if you refrigerate an open bottle of red, it will keep much longer, never mind the critics.

5. A glass of red wine a day keeps the doctor away. The chemical composition of the grape's skins -- resins, astringents, and antioxidants -- accounts for the healthy properties of wine.

A good wine need not be prohibitively expensive. In fact, a good wine need not be expensive at all. The May 2007 edition of Consumer Reports rated 10 wines, all under $10.00. Their list included cabernet sauvignons, chardonnays, merlots, pinot grigios, a riesling and a zinfandel. Among those cited were: Rosemount Estate shiraz-cabernet (Australia, 2004); Stone Cellars by Beringer (California, 2005, a chardonnay); Concha y Toro Casillero Del Diabolo (Chile, 2005, a merlot); Hogue Columbia Valley (Washington, 2005, a pinot grigio); Covey Run Columbia Valley (Washington, 2005, the Reisling); and Rancho Zabaco Dancing Bull (California, 2004, the zinfandel).

THE VINEYARD

Brady Hansen

SO YOU WANT TO OPEN A RESTAURANT?

What is a business? Something people will pay more for than you did. A waiter brings you a glass of water that costs the restaurant owner $0.60. This should get your attention!

Entering the marketplace is a challenge. Just when you think you have perfected your product, something exceeds your grasp. The future belongs to change. What you know now and what you learn tomorrow will determine success or failure.

The Greek philosopher Herodotus based his life work on the theory of change. A prominent modern business leader once said, "Change is a process, not an event." All successful enterprises are managed from that challenging assumption, and the world of food is no different. Thank you, F.J.

There exists one universal lesson in business: Be objective, see a clear reality. This is most difficult to do because ego and emotion are in everything. All successful people have been able to practice objective management. The practice works best in business settings where the product or service offered to the public is not as personal as food and wine. As we have said, food has a great personal meaning. A restaurant business recreates a family setting, which is subjective, and flies in the face of objective business practices. This notwithstanding, both must be served.

There are four challenges to operating a restaurant:

1. It is staffed by mostly young, temporary workers on their way to being something else.

2. The business operates at night, unnatural in a modern, family-structured society.

3. Picture whatever business you are in and imagine managing it when the norm is that your customers are drinking alcohol, eating and demanding attention.

4. Food is a commodity to which people feel they have a natural right, similar to the attitude concerning health care. The individual's right to food provided a major controversy during the Cold War when the United States withheld grain shipments to the Iron Curtain countries. The argument was simple: food should not be used as a weapon.

It is important to understand the reasons you want to be in the restaurant business. The best reason is that you get to do all the tasks yourself, which is in direct opposition to our modern business culture that stresses specialization. When you set the concept in motion and watch it grow, you get a direct experience. Few eateries can afford to hire professionals to perform the myriad functions inherent in running a restaurant. Ultimately, it is you who sets the business in motion, devises the strategy, hires the staff, specifies the tasks to be executed, and reaps the rewards or failures.

Know your reasons:

1. People are often in careers due to the influence of other people and personal circumstances. Do not let this happen, but if it does, you need to leave the business.

2. Some of the most common "wrong" reasons for being in the restaurant business are:

*   You love food and wine
*   You love people
*   The business is glamorous

There are a few rules to operating a successful restaurant, some of the most important are listed below:

1. Have confidence in yourself and that your concept will work.

2. Be aware that it is difficult to get accurate and sophisticated information from other restaurant operations (especially financial information). Also, the business world of financial services is geared mostly to serve medium to large businesses, not small ones.

3. The general observation of the restaurant business is that it's thriving because the dining room is half full and noisy. To make money, a restaurant must be full and busy seven days a week. Only on rare occasions do small (30-50 seats) restaurants work.

4. Almost any area in a city can work. However, people will travel a bit for an exceptional dining experience. In the suburbs or the country, the cliché, "Location "Location! Location!" is even truer than elsewhere. "Consistency! Consistency! Consistency!" comes in at a close second to The Location Rule.

5. Be aware that your personal concept may well have to be compromised. In business, quantity is as important as quality.

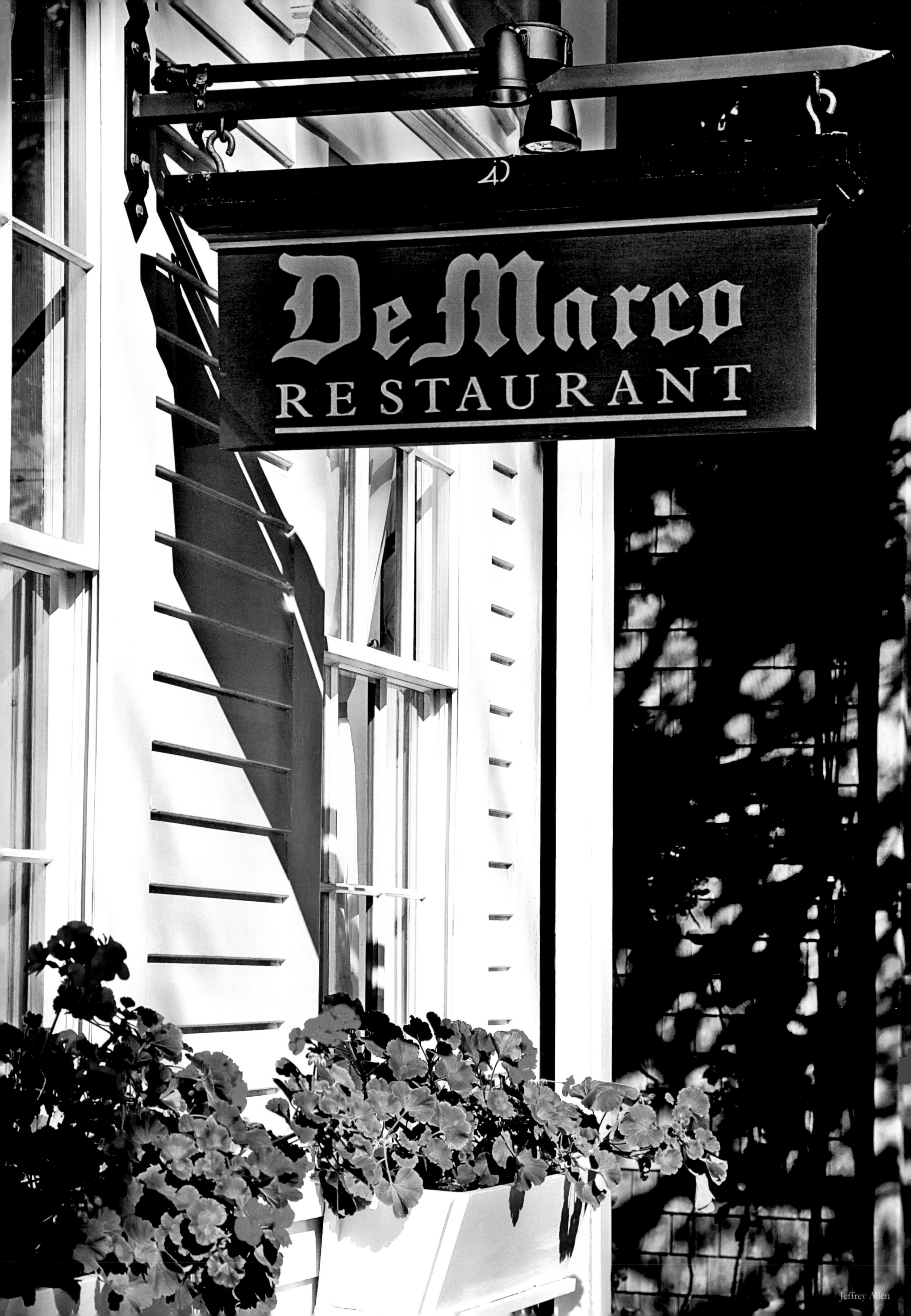

Jeffrey Allen

6. Accept practicing imperfection, but never lose sight of the ideal, the art of operating a fine dining enterprise is extraordinarily challenging and will defy perfection.

7. Theft is prevalent; it is so prevalent in the public's mind that the majority of conversations I have had with customers begin by asking me about it.

8. All bookkeeping, records and accounting should be done by a person independent of the restaurant operation and should report directly to the owner.

9. All politics are local as is your clientele and for the same reasons. This means that you should know your clientele, who they are, their socioeconomic status, and their expectations in food and wine. You can educate your clientele, but that will take a considerable amount of time.

10. Interview a prospective employee as you would for a large corporation. Make sure to go over every item on the resume. It is important to check past employers, references, dates, and wages. Restaurant managers hate calling references, but it must be done!

11. Be demanding but firm. Train people for success, but do not hesitate to dismiss if necessary.

12. Here are two of my favorite food writers who gave me lasting insights into the world of food: Waverly Root (The Food of France; The Food of Italy; Food) and MFK Fisher. (Consider the Oyster; With Bold Knife and Fork; How to Cook a Wolf; The Art of Eating; The Gastronomical Me.)

A WELL-RUN RESTAURANT

There are key components to running a good restaurant. Everything must be integrated, from the tiniest detail to the core of the business. It is important to set the scene: The environment created by the building and the décor is the first thing the customer notices. The person at the door should be a good ringmaster. He or she greets guests and lets them know they have entered a high energy environment. If you don't come from a family that loved having people visit, then you shouldn't work the front door of a restaurant, or for that matter in any business that requires making people feel welcome. The host or hostess should talk about the food and wine or recent events which begins to personalize the customer's experience. If customers have to wait for a table, keep them informed every few minutes;

it is vital that they feel you have not forgotten them.

To the public, service is just as important as the food. It sets the tone for the full enjoyment of the meal and ensures return visits. A talented server should gauge the customers' mood. Having judged the appropriateness of the moment, he or she should engage the guest with knowledge of the menu and the wine list. One comment I overheard from a waiter to an indecisive diner was, "Why not try two or three appetizers and one entrée?" In this way, the server acts as the liaison between the desire of the patron and the product.

When a restaurant hits its rhythm and everything is running properly, the customer enters into that milieu with high anticipation and leaves well satisfied. The behavior that diners convey to their fellow diners is infectious. After 28 years at De Marco, many customers know and greet each other, resulting in a club-like atmosphere. When diners are happy, it creates a charged ambiance throughout the restaurant.

BUILDING DEMARCO RESTAURANT
-The First 25 Years

The "Great Fire" of Nantucket occurred on July 13, 1846. It burned the majority of the downtown area, including the bulk of its commercial buildings, to the ground. Along Pearl Street, later to become known as India Row, a number of residences were lost, among them number 9, where De Marco Restaurant now stands, the tenth occupant of these premises.

After purchasing the property in the summer of 1977, my brothers Dave, Denny, and I immediately set out to do an authentic restoration through research and the advice from master builders, including the late Bruce Killen, a dedicated Nantucketer and builder. We gutted the entire three-story structure to bare bones. We insulated the entire building, including special sound insulation between floors. All new infrastructures were installed, as were 23 steel columns in the basement and a steel beam through the entire center of the building. We were dedicated to completing the restoration with materials consistent with the period of original construction. The new support beams (12 feet long and 12" by 12" wide) were purchased from an old sawmill being torn down in Shrewsbury, Massachusetts.

The complete restoration took three years and, as is the case with most renovation projects of this magnitude, cost more than imagined. Completing the restoration and securing the necessary approvals would take another year. I therefore decided to rent the first floor of the property to an ice cream and card shop (currently operating in Manhattan) for the summer season of 1978.

Within the first two weeks of their opening, a reporter from the local newspaper in Nantucket, The Inquirer and Mirror, telephoned me in New York City about a letter written by a Nantucket attorney to the editor, entitled "The Rot from Within." The letter stated that Don DeMarco had opened a soft porn shop! Unbeknownst to me, the tenant had set up a business in the heart of Nantucket's historic district selling edible chocolate genitalia and flasher dolls along with other assorted soft porn paraphernalia. At the very time I was scheduled to appear before the board of selectmen for approval, I was being associated with a soft porn merchant!

The tenant had a lease that lasted until August. I immediately began legal proceedings to evict him, an undertaking that took longer than the term of the lease. As a result of this mess, I was requested by the late Reverend Metters to appear before the Nantucket Civic League regarding my intentions. They informed me that rumor had it I was planning to open a discothèque with some partners from Boston. I assured them that I had no partners and that we planned to open a fine-dining restaurant, and nothing more. This was when I wholeheartedly sped up the process and developed what it is today -- the second-oldest restaurant on the island still run by its original owner. At the present writing, Nantucket has about 70 eateries.

The original financing was difficult, as was the time delay involved in the opening. Banks did not favor lending money to new restaurant operations, therefore, most of my financing came from individuals. This was at a time when national economic policy had driven interest rates to over 20%. All of my financing was short-term with one loan as high as 26%. Major problems arose at our first hearing for a liquor license, which was refused. The second attempt, while approved by a vote of 3 to 2 margin, was later amended to require our closing by 10 pm-- an impossible requirement for a complete fine-dining operation. Writing about these events today it all seems humorous, but the risk was real, and the process was portrayed in a musical revue, titled Nantucket Restaurant.

First performed in 1983 at a sit-down dinner for 125 invited guests in Nantucket at the Point Breeze Hotel, parodied the approval process. It was a celebration (our 4th year) to say thank you for an initial success. Some of the lyrics are as follows:

Petitioner (before the Board of Selectmen): I want to open a restaurant!

Selectmen:

He wants to open a restaurant.

Who does he think he is?

Starts with a flutter flutter

And it grows in to a mutter mutter

It will drive you round the bend though

When it rises to crescendo

That mutter mutter

Of the cacaphonic stutter

Of the Yankee tut tut tutter

The tut tut tutter in a strut strut strut strutter

And the mutt mutt mutter

Of who else the abutte

I am one of the selectmen

Yes we are selectman

When our forefathers came here they loved these holy acres

They wasted Wampanoag

Then set fire to the Quakers

They left us a heritage of thrift and purity

But today we have the welfare state and social security

Petitioner:

Who are you guys?

Selectmen:

For we are the selectman

Proverbially correct men

Invariably direct men

You cannot suspect men

Who are your selectmen

Once that you select men

To be your selectmen

You do not reject men

It's foolish to collect men

only to eject men

You're pretty much perfect men

in effect selectmen

Petitioner:

I'll need a sign.

Selectmen:

You may need a variance

And to get a variance

You must be Aryan

Oh, a sign will be fine

In inches six by nine

But it can't be on a line

With the sea or the bay

Or a road, or a pine

Or on a pole in a hole

But if your goal is a sign

Don't say wine or even dine

See by law eighty nine

When our forefathers came here

They loved the woods and the wetlands

We've established by laws so you cannot get land

Building permit, parking permit

Microphone permit, kitchen permit

Store license, liquor license,

Entertainment license, license, license

We don't care for tourists or their vile habits

They disturb the chipmunks

And annoy the rabbits

They bring in the money

But we all our wishing

That our little island

Would go back to fishing

We've had it with the Portuguese who came here in the battalions

We don't need the Irish or the North Italians

The world is full of ideas, only a few become realities. There is no perfect formula, only the ability to apply talent. There are no secret recipes or business plans; there is only execution and the joy of it. Thank you, P.B. Finding a cure for cancer, eliminating hunger, despair and violence are perfect ideals, but yet to be accomplished.

Like all businesses, execution is the key. Getting a thing done and making it work provides a complete experience of the hands-on process. Strategy and theory should not be overemphasized; they are necessary for a beginning and will evolve and mature as the plan progresses.

The concept of research and high science, including the food arts, revolves around hard won solutions. Everything in the world is integrated, we just don't know how. We come to the earth made from the stuff of stars, as does everything we eat and drink. What wisdom we attain in this life comes from the origins of the universe. Growing, preparing, and consuming food are among the most human of all endeavors. This may be threatened today by our ever-expanding global consumption.

DeM

CHEFS

The first generation was by necessity; the second generation is by choice.

I conceived the idea for DeMarco Restaurant after I was introduced to a former teacher of Renaissance literature, who, while studying in Florence, took a cooking class to get away from the library. He loved it so he became a chef. What resulted was our restaurant (1979) rigorously dedicated to replicating the foods of northern Italy and to reviving the highest standards of excellence--an ethic whose cultural foundation originated in Tuscany.

Some historians have said that there are two original kitchens in the world: Chinese and Mediterranean. DeMarco's northern Italian cuisine is the cuisine of the Renaissance, the wellspring of modern Western culture. The foods of Tuscany, the wines of Piedmont; meals that once graced the table of the Medicis.

DeMarco Restaurant brings to its clientele an up-to-date classicism. This is apparent in the ways in which principles of preparation, presentation, service, and environment have been reinterpreted and applied to the needs and expectations of the contemporary American customer. In short, it is a continuing effort to create the ideal.

In 1979, DeMarco was one of the few restaurants that made its own fresh pasta, fresh Tuscan breads, and fresh desserts. The American chefs, while concerned with authenticity, were also willing to experiment in order to adapt the cuisine to contemporary lifestyles (the concern with health issues), and tastes, (using fresh ingredients that have been refined and improved over time). One of the many adaptations is the creamless cream sauce. See page 80.

Another good example of culinary adaptation is a dish called umido de pesce, a delicate Italian bouillabaisse. It has no added salt, little fat or cholesterol, and a moderate number of calories. The requisite olive-oil-based rouille that finishes the dish has been reduced from four or five tablespoons of oil to only one, with negligible effect on taste. This recipe was featured in the New York Times Living Section February 15, 1984 cover story, titled "In New Restaurant Dishes, Health and Good Taste".

A generation ago, the vast majority of cooks and chefs began working in restaurants as teenage trainees (often washing dishes) and graduated to higher-level positions in a commercial kitchen. Hard-working and street-smart, they did not have the advantage of a higher education, and therefore learned through the traditional European system of apprenticeship.

Today, that has changed along with the rest of the industry, popularized by a host of television shows glamorizing and elevating the chef's stature to a high social status, a level that previously did not exist in America. Their great contribution to food in America has gone even further -- celebrity -- a position that historically only Europeans enjoyed. With respect to their food, European chefs no longer hold a vast advantage over American chefs. Americans, through work, study and travel, have caught up with their European mentors and counterparts, as Americans always do. Historically, American workers have acquired a process, (if they didn't actually invent it) and over time, learned to produce a state-of-the-art product. We are facing the problem today—global competition and outsourced labor, and much of the American way of life depends on its outcome!

After an expensive culinary education and an unpaid internship, the young graduates often feel a bit disillusioned when they realize how much time and how little compensation their near future will entail. A restaurant of their own -- the dream of every young chef -- must usually be deferred for many years, given the required experience and capital.

A chef exercises a profession unlike any other: a shoemaker, carpenter or investment banker, all have the opportunity to work one-on-one with their customers. The problem is exacerbated by the fact that chefs are so busy that they usually do not have time during the labor-intense service hours to listen to anything except the orders.

Some chefs cannot take criticism of any kind, and the service staff may become reluctant to speak to them. This situation cannot be tolerated. All customers' compliments as well as complaints must be communicated to management immediately. The lack of direct interaction, which is imperative in most small businesses, can be partially compensated for by succinct communication between the service staff and the kitchen staff, something akin to a real-time message service. Twenty-five staff members dedicated to pleasing 200 customers for six hours every night is an immense challenge. Every staff member must maintain a personal rapport with every customer. Even during the busiest of times, they must strive to keep business personal.

The food, of course, is what diners come for. The taste that lingers is why they come back. Yet food is truly enhanced by its presentation. Chefs prefer large plates upon which to present their fare, similar to artists who paint large canvases. The white china plate particularly lends itself to the chef's creative talent. However, the business of being a chef is a disjointed endeavor, since chefs are in the kitchen usually hidden away from the end user in the dining room. They rarely see the customer, and therefore never hear the real-time reactions to the food that they have so skillfully prepared. Diners' comments are fascinating and instructive, as any waiter will tell you.

Jeffrey Allen

The everyday dichotomy between the service staff and the kitchen staff must be integrated as a business, or lose efficiency. This is no different than what must be done in large businesses, which often struggle to integrate research, manufacturing with marketing and sales. Nothing is more important than creating and preserving the one-on-one feeling in the restaurant business.

One of the other very helpful exercises in solving the problem of communication between the front and the back of the house, and the appreciation for the others' jobs, is to have servers come into the kitchen an hour before service to help out with food preparation and simple kitchen tasks. Also on a weekly basis, servers should prepare a short lecture on their favorite foods and wines (on the menu) with the chefs present.

The food industry has been in the forefront of creating opportunity for women and minorities, while providing a good living for those pursuing other careers. The massive entry of women in the workforce beginning in the 1970s has allowed many of them to get to the top levels of corporate America. Many women in America have become famous and wealthy as chefs, restaurant owners, and media personalities. In Europe, especially in France, however, it is still fairly rare to find women in fine dining restaurant kitchens.

In the 28-year history of chefs at DeMarco, women have always been an integral part of the kitchen. DeMarco is one of the few restaurants of any kind--French, Italian, or American--that has had women as chefs from the beginning, doing the actual cooking. It is also one of the few that has a majority of women on the service and management staff. To the extent we have been successful, training has been key; such as daily meetings, where the service staff tastes the food and learns the ingredients of the specials. It is our standard practice to have chefs and managers discuss the preparations for the evening and the wines that will complement them. For the staff, a family meal is eaten together every night, creating a camaraderie as they prepare for their night's business.

Frequent trips to Italy, sometimes with staff and friends--to be decadent, to eat and drink the best you can twice a day--is part of a never-ending education. We have many friends in Italy who are chefs, and others who operate vineyards; and they love to talk about food and wine. There is a tremendous cultural influence from the Mediterranean that drives much of the American culinary enterprise.

In the restaurant business, you come to know your colleagues very well. Restaurants, however, may be a little different because they function at night, and socializing is influenced by food and wine. It is perhaps most like theater. Waiters set the stage for an audience of diners; the staff are the actors in the performance. There has always been an interactive dynamic between servers and diners.

Sadly, on two separate occasions, we have had the funerals of two good friends and long-term employees. But the gathering bore witness to the great tribute paid these young deceased people from their restaurant friends. Because of the longevity of their employment, friends (alumni) renewing acquaintances and some meeting for the first time, were moved to ask, "What summer did you work there?" It felt almost like a college reunion, festive and alive, all due to the humanity, the mentoring, and the good times these two wonderful young people had created. Even now, colleagues from that period return and hear for the first time of their friends' passing and discuss the good times.

Today, as we look to these youthful, idealistic people and their band of friends for leadership in the new century, I would like to tell their parents; if they could see them as I do, separate and apart, doing what they taught them, giving what they gave them; inspired, hard-working, and often adored by their customers, their parents would love them even more, if that is possible.

Brian

Lawrence

Douglas

Denny DeMarco

Chris   Our Managers   Julia

Niall

Our youthful and spirited staff, which includes some exceptionally gifted people, makes every evening seem as though they were getting ready to perform a play, one that goes on every night. The pre-dinner hour has a rhythmic routine that is both frantic and joyful, in anticipation of what the night will bring. The staff's higher education, curiosity and worldly pursuits create a respect for each other, the benefits of which are conveyed directly to the food, the wine and the customers. Lasting friendships have developed among these colleagues, as well as between customers and staff. One of our employees set a record --12 years working consecutive summers.

BARTENDERS

Bartenders are among the most interesting professionals in our culture. They often provide a home away from home; a patron knows he will almost always have good company and good conversation. Most bartenders are articulate, streetwise, sports enthusiasts, and politically opinionated. They can also be the coordinator, the social director and the advisor for a large following. Bartenders understand human nature and are the best unpaid psychiatrists in the world.

The difference between a good cocktail and a mediocre one is easy to detect. One can tell whether the bartender took pains to produce the right product, or whether he or she just went through the motions. Our favorite bartender in New York, J.J. Featherstone, when shaking a drink, takes on a concentrated stance, assumes an attitude similar to that of a professional athlete--feet squarely planted, body erect, shaker held over the right shoulder with two hands in a rapid, exacting motion. It is a joy to see.

A bartender plays a key role in relating to customers; he or she is a huge factor in the popularity and the energy level of the cocktail area, which can affect the entire restaurant.

Bartenders were also parodied in the musical, New York-Nantucket Tavern 2002 in a song. The lyrics are as follows:

Bartenders are the loneliest people in the world

I'm confessor to everyone, psychiatrist to some, mother and father to them all.

I've been through five thousand divorces, fourteen thousand affairs and a million other despairs

And my girl has to sit over there just a bit, no time for us to be a grand part of it.

She sits there all alone our conversations cut off by the wail and the call

"Bartender! Bartender! Bartender!"

True I like my position, it suits my disposition.

My council is sought, not part of the crowd.

But they all come to see me, some rich and some bleeding,

All shapes and all sizes, my clamoring multitude.

I don't have all the answers, I'm tired of their questions, the look in their eyes.

And I want to leave…I could just leave…

DeM

While bars have been known for being dens of iniquity, indignant teetotaler rampages, and the sites of infamous brawls, they are also places of intellectual gatherings and starting points for some of the most famous pages of history. A savvy barkeep doesn't just mix good drinks, he knows how to make good conversation, too, at appropriate times. As the bartender observes in New York-Nantucket Musical, "Daniel Webster once remarked that the tavern was the headquarters of the American Revolution. Who knows?! The Boston Tea Party may have been plotted at the Green Dragon Tavern or in any tavern up and down the East Coast. Possibly even on Broadway in New York City's very own Burns Tavern. Good ol' Thomas Jefferson wrote part of the Declaration of Independence at NYC's Indian Queen Tavern. And Washington delivered an emotional farewell at Fraunces Tavern. Where did the idea of free assembly and speech begin? In Greece? Probably even before that! Perhaps, the modern New England Town Meetings (including Nantucket) are directly descended from these historical tavern assemblies."

On another occasion, I overheard our longtime friend and bartender, a brilliant and highly politically-minded individual, passionately conversing with customers. "Where are the great leaders of the world today? Like Gandhi, Mandela, and Mother Teresa?" he asked his attentive audience. "With all of the education, sophistication, and communication worldwide, what happens to all the young talent that doesn't rise up to lead the world?" This kind of discourse, followed by a mundane food remark, made virtually the very next minute, demonstrates the range of discourse in the restaurant business.

At the time of this writing, the just-published and immensely readable, informative book, The Joy of Drinking by Barbara Holland, takes up the cause. Drinking, she writes, is "the social glue of the human race." It takes time and patience, getting to know the bartender, as well as the "regulars" who have the tendency to view a newcomer with some skepticism. The neighborhood bar is a microcosm, and its inhabitants generally have a solid sense of territorial rights.

Jeffrey Allen

BAR TALK: REAL AND IMAGINED

The following is an excerpt from New York-Nantucket Tavern produced in New York in 2002:

The Scene: People gathered around a bar.

Nantucketer: You're not going to believe this! My garbage wasn't being picked up for weeks, so I asked the truck driver why? He said, in a snooty voice, "your garbage is all the wrong shape, the wrong color, it's from all the wrong stores. Here in Nantucket, we're used to designer trash. The boxes must at least come from Neiman Marcus or Bloomingdale's. See the motto on our truck? "If you can't use it, neither can we!"

New Yorker: Wait until you hear this one. You know that CEO that comes here all the time? He was complaining about a business deal he worked on all weekend, but fell apart on Monday. I asked how much would you make on a deal like that in a weekend? He told me 10 million dollars!

Nantucketer: Wow? I know people that have to work a whole year for 10 million dollars!

Brooklyn-New Yorker: I'm New York tough, ready & rough. I live in the city. Where a Nantucket guy couldn't survive, I thrive!

Nantucketer: Survive? We work in the wild winds. Hail and snow. Ever see a Northeaster blow? I'm a Nantucket guy, courtly & brave. Oh, my sweet friend, harken to me. Do you realize that, from this little island, our forebears ruled three quarters of the whaling oceans?

Brooklyn-New Yorker: Forget about it!

Nantucketer: We were part of the Underground Railroad. And when the slave owners came to Nantucket to get their slaves back, the Quakers told them no! They had to turn around the very same day!

New Yorker: Yeah. That's because they couldn't afford to stay overnight!

Nantucketer: I can't get into Sankaty no matter what my pedigree – so I took myself to one of the new clubs in town – you know what they said? We don't care about pedigree, show me the money!

A FOREIGN POLICY LESSON IN NANTUCKET

It occurred to me years after the beginning of our restaurant operation (1979) that young Latin American, Irish, Caribbean and most recently the Eastern Europeans, were all excellent workers; they couldn't do a bad job. I'd be hard-pressed to think of an instance in 28 years where one of them was irresponsible, inadequate, or lazy. The vast majority were strong, solid, and it was a pleasure to work with them. When given a task, they are a joy to watch—their riveted concentration of dedicated energy, as though finding themselves, delighted to prove their worth, self-assured in an alien land. We were all part of that at one time!

Slowly, a light goes on: It's not the people of undeveloped countries that created negative stereotypes, but the fact that they have never been given a real opportunity to prove themselves in their own country. They are ambitious, intelligent and hardworking. All these guest workers ever needed was a level playing field, and they would have produced goods and services as they do in Nantucket and other resorts. Witness today the dynamic advent of globalization driven by a labor force from developing countries. The once-large, young Irish population dwindled in Nantucket after the European Union invested heavily in Ireland and created a competitive wage, and it all occurred in the span of 20 years.

Corrupt governments kept their citizens downtrodden without real opportunity, hope or a future for their families. All things being equal a human being will grasp a real opportunity. It is especially tragic today as modern economic methods and technology are available to almost everyone. These guest workers of Nantucket taught us this lesson long ago.

For 28 years, our restaurant has been the meeting place for staff members and customers. Many have developed life-long friendships with each other; some have married, and some have chosen to live in Nantucket permanently.

Every season is an eclectic mix of the new and the old. The many people who flock to the island during the busy season mix seamlessly with those who return summer after summer and those who reside on the island year-round, all relishing the Nantucket experience. They fall in love with the island and often desire to live there. Working and living the Nantucket experience is a microcosm of American history.

At the same time, island life can make one feel a bit like an expat, completely secluded in the cobblestone world of Main Street, surrounded by ferry boats and water. It is a life found only on islands, and those of New England, especially Nantucket, hold a special place in our hearts.

Nantucket! Take out your map and look at it. See what a real corner of the world it occupies!"

- Herman Melville, Moby Dick

Nantucket Shore

Water spreads to its thinnest limits

In perfect half-crests, mark and map the shore

Proving earth is round.

The quite peaceful display

Nantucket Sound

DeM

DeM

THE CUSTOMER
and
THE WAITER

The vast majority of customers in our 28-year history have been gracious, interesting, and a complete joy to serve. A multitude of relationships are renewed every year, made brighter by the unique cycle of winter abstinence. A restaurant develops a personality and attracts people of like kind. Given the test of time, it becomes a bit of an institution. It is not by accident but design that people who form life long friendships come from a strong family background.

The customer was also parodied in the musical, the opening lyric, sung by a waiter, "Service not servitude, I like my job, don't you be rude..."

The public will forgive anything except indifference. This is the theme of the speech I give at the beginning of every season. The challenging corollary to this is, in the landscape of the public arena, the unpleasant do sometimes gather.

One of the many positive things about the modern era as compared to the past is that service no longer means abuse. Those historic horrible conditions were demeaning and brutal, because of this service took on a rather bad name. Some positions, however, were considered quite prestigious, such as the coveted post of the refined English butler. The modern waiter (now preferably called server) should be modeled on that concept; professional, solicitous and informed.

Service jobs are considered menial too much of the American work force. It is one of the reasons globalization has blossomed. Our forebears, who labored in America at the turn of the century, gave the succeeding generations their skilled and prosperous status. Today, most American commercial kitchens are primarily staffed with foreign guest workers. From harvest to the final processing, the food service industry in the United States has over 12.5 million employees, making it the largest employer after the federal government.

The ability to motivate a young, sophisticated adult attending a $40,000-a-year university, and create a professional service mentality is a constant challenge to a seasonal restaurant business. A lot of trial and error go into accomplishing this at a professional level.

One has only to think about your last encounter at a restaurant or some other retail entity when the service was unsatisfactory. I have seen it happen in the past and had to put a stop to it very quickly. One such case was when a waiter complained to the customer about the amount of the tip, which he clearly indicated in no uncertain terms was inadequate. Needless to say, his services were no longer required, "effective immediately." I also had occasion to fire a waiter for outrageous behavior toward H.C., whose family is one of our oldest and dearest customers. The customer had made a polite request, and was rudely told by the waiter that he was too busy, and if he didn't like it he could leave.

There exists a great pride in these young people that can be tapped into by teaching them the good side of customer service, and of course, a way to earn good money. When management takes its work seriously, it inspires the entire staff, which is directly experienced by the customer. This very human process is the single most rewarding in the restaurant business.

HANDLING COMPLAINTS

To do this well may take me another 25 years of practice. The world is full of givers and takers, heavily weighted by takers. When dealing with customer complaints, I have learned to discern whether I was dealing with ordinary, legitimate dissatisfaction or some underlying unreasonableness from individuals who will never be satisfied.

On a busy summer night a few years ago, I volunteered to work at the door (our hostess was ill) and my wife, Therese, was kind enough to help me seat people, her first time to do so. I was called away for a moment to the upstairs dining room. When I returned, Therese had a shocked look on her face. I asked what happened and she pointed to a man waiting in the bar area. He had an Alfred Hitchcock profile with curly white hair and a splendid sartorial presence, with him an elegant well dressed lady. After being told that without a reservation, he would have to wait at the bar and that we would try to seat him as soon as possible, he announced to my wife, in a metallic, high-pitched, clipped British accent, "OUTRAGEOUS! ABSOLUTELY OUTRAGEOUS!!" He continued, as loud as an angry Shakespearean actor, "TOTAL INCOMPETENCE!"

He nevertheless returned the next night, this time with a reservation, but did not like the table we had allotted him. He repeated his declaration of "outrageous incompetence," for everyone to hear, and unbelievably walked over to the table he wanted and stood there while the seated customers were still dining. I asked him to leave. He did not, but instead waited at the bar indeterminately for his desired table.

An instance of a more rational request comes to mind when, early one August evening, a French woman, looking very haggard and accompanied by three young children, hesitantly opened the door. She asked in near despair, "Do you know where I can bring my children?" to which I replied, "Right here is fine. We have always welcomed children." Nantucket is a family vacation resort and should welcome and cater to families as much as possible.

SCENES AT THE DOOR

Early in the evening, when we first open the restaurant, I am often standing with the hostess at the door, watching people walk by, peruse the outside menu, and continue on. This is at 6 pm, when availability for seating is usually wide open. Privately we wish that all of the people who stop to read the menu would come in. I often joke with the hostess or the maitre d' of the night, saying, "It's your job to get those people in here!" Of course, there's nothing one can do, and for many years, whichever hostess I was addressing always knew that I was kidding.

A few years ago, however, on one of these pleasant evenings, I remarked to the young, smart, attractive hostess as we observed a distinguished-looking couple stop in front to look at the menu, that it was her job to entice them to come in. Immediately, she opened the door, stepped down to talk quietly to them and returned a few moments later with the couple in tow. I was pleasantly surprised, but whispered to her, "You can't do that!" Her response, and the moral of this vignette is this: "If you don't go out and talk to them, they won't come in!" After years of trying…it took her a moment! Thank you, CG.

Another-observed and rather amusing occurrence, possibly unique to Nantucket, is when arriving without a reservation the would-be customer declares, "But I've been coming to Nantucket for twenty years!!!" I have yet to understand why this would help them secure a table.

The reservation system in a busy resort restaurant is a constant challenge. We are inundated daily with the desires of well-meaning customers to change times, the number of people in the party, and special menu requests. Then there are those not-so-well-meaning people who pretend they have made a reservation and have not done so. When obliged to turn down a customer's request our staff has been trained to say, "We are very sorry, we cannot accommodate you." The only thing a restaurant can do that is worse than turning down a customer is to take them and do a poor job.

On one occasion, a customer who was asked to wait ten minutes asked haughtily, "Why do I have to wait ten minutes?" I replied, "as a matter of fact, you don't." Most people are understanding about waiting for a table, but some others think they are being treated badly and revert to immature behavior, despite the fact that they are center stage in a public place. Raising their voice and abusing staff members are favorite tactics.

THE ART OF THE QUICK DRAW OR HOW TO AVOID PAYING THE BILL

This is a maneuver performed at a dining table when someone (usually a man) offers to pay for the bill only after it is in the hand of another patron at the table. The Quick Draw occurs while still seated and requires a movement of the hand from table level to the wallet in lightning-quick, Western-gunfighter style. The hand never actually reaches the wallet; it stops, frozen in midair.

Another version of how to avoid paying the bill occurred when a celebrity called me over after a large, expensive birthday party celebration. Standing in a corner, he offered to pay the bill and searched desperately in all his pockets for his credit card.. After much effort, reminiscent of a game of charades, further rumpling his already crumpled cloths, he abandoned the search. As he walked away, the credit card fell from his clothing. I picked it up and handed it to him. I understood he never intended to pay the bill.

On another occurrence, a party of twelve dined all evening and gave the waiter trouble the entire time. The waiter held his tongue. Once apprised of the situation, I approached them and they turned their abuse on me. I asked them to leave. Their dinner was complete except for dessert. They said they would not pay the bill (assuming a certain leverage?) to which I replied firmly to all, "Don't pay, get up and go." Fortunately, this was the only time such an incident happened.

Don & Dave DeMarco

NOTE ABOUT ACCOLADES

Of the many personal compliments and published reviews we
have received during our 28 year history, one stands out in my
mind above all others... even if it is not really true. A frequent
diner from the Midwest declared in the middle of our reception
area, "this is the best restaurant in the world, I know because I sell
airplanes around the world!"

RECILPES

I often disregard recipes and have paid the price for not following them, but clearly the rewards outweigh the failures. I only cook at home. Sometimes a recipe is a one-time thing, not to be duplicated again, a creation of the moment like a great golf shot, a true adventure every time.

It would be impossible to present all the recipes and their variations in this book—they number in the hundreds—but here are some of our customers' favorites, over the last 28-years.

Sometimes a recipe is a one-time thing, not to be duplicated or experienced in exactly the same way again—a creation of the moment like a great golf shot, not for the faint of heart. It is an adventure when you don't know how a dish is going to come out, even if you've made some variation of it many times before! Cooking, after all, is a creative endeavor, a true adventure every time.

Jeffrey Allen

SEAFOOD SALAD

This can be served as a **perfect** summer-time appetizer or as a main course. Keep in mind that the dried cod should be soaked in frequently changed fresh water for at least 24 hours before preparing the salad.

8 green lip mussels
12 Prince Edward Island mussels
15 little neck clams
15 cockles
1 shallot sliced
2 cloves garlic sliced
1 large tomato diced
1/2 cup chiffonade basil
1/2 cup dry white wine
1 tbsp. olive oil
1 loaf of crusty bread

Heat a large. sauté pan over high heat, add shallots and garlic sauté until soft and just starting to color.

Pull pan off the heat to avoid flames and add little necks and cockles tomatoes and white wine and cover with a tight fitting lid.

After about 2 minutes add the PEI mussels and recover for about 1 minute, finally add the green lip mussels and heat through.
When all the shell fish has opened divide them evenly between four bowls with the liquid that is in the bottom of the pan. Sprinkle the basil evenly around the top of the shell fish, and serve with the bread. *Serves 4*

SOYBEANS WITH TASTE

It took a long time to figure out how to make whole soybeans taste good. However they are so **healthy** that it was worth the effort. The key to it is cooking them with other beans that easily take on a flavor (soybeans do not). The result is a vegetarian entrée whose rich taste truly is a surprise. Serve in large bowls with oven-toasted garlic bread.

1/2 cup chopped red onion, finely chopped
3 large cloves garlic, minced
4 cups broth (vegetable, beef, fish or chicken, preferably low sodium)
1/2 cup soybeans
1/3 cup kidney beans
1/3 cup white navy beans
1/4 cup barley
2 tbsp. honey
1/2 tsp fennel seeds
1/2 tsp. ground black pepper
1/4 cup chopped chives
1/2 tsp whole black peppercorns
1/4 cup chopped white raisins
Thick slices of oven-toasted garlic bread.

Wash, rinse and soak all the beans in a large pot of water over night. In a saucepan, sauté the onion and garlic until soft but not brown, and set aside. Drain the soaked beans, cover with water, and cook for 1 hour. Next, add the sautéed onion and garlic, the broth, peppercorns and fennel seeds to the pot and cook over medium heat for 45 minutes. Add the barley, chives, honey and white raisins and cook for an additional 45 minutes. Ladle in large bowls with oven-toasted garlic bread. *Serves 4-6.*

Note: If you are using precooked, canned beans, rinse thoroughly and do not add until the end of the 45-minute cooking time.

EARTHY MUSHROOM SOUP

A soup for **all seasons**, this one tastes good no matter what the weather.

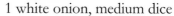

1 white onion, medium dice
2 tbsp. olive oil
1 bunch sage, leaves only, chopped.
1 bunch mint, chopped.
4 cloves of garlic, minced
4 lb. portabella mushrooms, cleaned and diced
1/2 lb. cleaned and sliced cremini mushrooms
1/2 lb. shitake mushrooms, cleaned, de-stemmed and sliced
1 Russet potato, peeled and diced
Sea salt and black pepper to taste

In a large saucepan over medium to high heat, sauté onions in olive oil until soft. Add sage, mint and garlic and cook for five minutes. Add mushrooms and sweat for five minutes. Add potatoes and enough water to submerge them. Bring to a boil, then reduce to low heat. Simmer for about 30 minutes, or until potatoes are cooked. Allow to cool. In a food processor, purée all the ingredients until smooth.

Let the mixture cool, then puree in a food processor. Adjust seasoning to taste. *Serves 6.*

ARTICHOKE-FILLED ENDIVE WITH ALMONDS

This **elaborate** appetizer is not easily prepared, but it is so delicious that it is worth the time to do so. We served it for very special occasions.

For the endive:
1 large artichoke, steamed, stripped of its leaves
24 endive leaves, washed dried, 12 left whole and 12 cut in half
Fresh lemon juice
Honey
1/4 cup finely chopped mint
White pepper to taste
Fennel, shaved into fine shreds, and coated in warm, unsalted butter
40 whole almonds, lightly toasted, then halved horizontally

For the garnish:
Crème fraîche, slightly sweetened with honey
Red currents to garnish
Sea salt and pepper to taste

With a teaspoon, scoop off the flesh of the steamed artichoke leaves and pile on a plate. Salt and pepper to taste and set aside. Squeeze each endive leaf with fresh lemon juice. Coat the endive leaves with honey, then dust with chopped mint and white pepper. Cover each endive leaf with a layer of shaved fennel. Preferably with a small pastry bag, top the shaved fennel with a thin layer of the artichoke flesh. Lightly press the halved almonds end to end on each endive leaf until entirely covered. Place halved endive leaves on top, and repeat for a second layer until all the endive leaves are completed. Arrange three to a plate. Add a dollop of crème fraîche on top. Sprinkle with red currants and garnish with mint sprigs. *Serves 4.*

DIVER SCALLOPS WITH BACON AND SAFFRON RISOTTO

Nothing conjures up the **love of the sea** and briny breezes more than shellfish, and scallops are no exception. No wonder Botticelli's Venus emerges from its beautiful shell.

12 sea scallops
12 thinly sliced bacon slices
2 yellow peppers diced
1 cup diced white onion
1 clove sliced garlic
1 cup Arborio rice
1 1/2 cups white wine
4 cups chicken stock (may not use all)
1 pinch saffron
Salt and pepper to taste
Extra virgin olive oil as needed

Wrap scallops in bacon and secure with a toothpick. Place scallops on a dinner plate cover with plastic wrap and reserve in the refrigerator.

In a tablespoon of olive oil, sauté ¼ cup of the onion and garlic until translucent (no color). Next, add ½ cup of white wine and reduce slowly over med- low heat until the liquid is evaporated. Add the peppers and sweat until they are soft (again no color). Add enough chicken stock to just cover peppers and cook for 10 to 15 minutes on med low heat.

Puree the pepper mixture in a blender and strain through a fine mesh sieve and gently press the solids through with a ladle or the back of a spoon. Discard the solids from inside the sieve and reserve the stained liquid in the refrigerator until needed
Steep saffron in remaining chicken stock over low heat.
In a medium sized pot over med high heat and add olive oil the rest of the onions a pinch of salt and sauté (stirring constantly to avoid burning the onions) until soft and translucent. Add the rice and toast until aromatic about 5 to 10 minutes.

Add the remaining white wine and stirring constantly to avoid sticking and to bring out the starches in the rice.

Once the wine has been absorbed add one cup of the chicken stock saffron infusion and stir until fully absorbed. Repeat until the rice is al dente or desired consistency and adjust seasoning with salt and pepper.

The rice should be very creamy like porridge. Cover and set aside in a warm place

Season the scallops with salt and pepper. Go easy on the salt because the bacon around the scallop is already a little salty. Heat a sauté pan with a tbls. of olive oil when pan is very hot but not smoking add the scallops being careful not to over crowd the pan. You may need to use more than one pan or work in batches. Crisp the bacon first for about 20 seconds per side. Sear the ends for about 30 seconds per side and set aside on a plate lined with a paper towel.

In 4 serving bowls place about ½ a cup of risotto, three scallops, and drizzle the pepper coulis around the outside of the rice. *Serves 4*

Jeffrey Allen

TRICOLOR SALAD

The colors in this salad are as **bright and fresh** as a flag whipping in a stiff sea breeze.

1 small ciabatta loaf or any other crusty bread, thinly sliced
 Extra virgin olive oil for brushing the crostini and for dressing
1/2 cup walnuts
1 red bell pepper
1 yellow bell pepper
1 head radicchio
1 yellow endive
1 lb. bag baby spinach

1/4 cup olive oil
1/8 cup Sherry vinegar
1/4 cup parmesan cheese
Sea salt and pepper to taste

Preheat oven to 350 degrees

To make crostini (long croutons) brush bread with olive oil and bake for about 10-15 min; let cool. Toast walnuts and let cool. Slice the bell pepper, radicchio and endive. In a bowl, mix the spinach, radicchio, endive and peppers. Dress the salad with olive oil, vinegar, salt and fresh ground pepper.

Garnish with crostini, Parmesan cheese, and walnuts. *Serves 4.*

PORCINI AND ONION PUDDING TART

Eating is a way to of **absorbing** the produce of the good earth into your body. Even sitting down to dine at a restaurant is a **natural** experience and nothing exudes the taste of the earth like mushrooms do.

For the filling:
1 lb. dried porcini mushrooms, reconstituted, chopped
3/4 lb sweet Vidalia onions, finely chopped
1/2 cup water
1 tbsp. lemon zest
3 whole eggs
1/2 cup of whole milk
1/4 cup sugar
1/2 cup dried black currants, reconstituted
1/4 cup light rum
Tart shells or small ramekins

Preheat oven to 350 degrees.

Reconstitute the dried porcini mushrooms for 1/2 hour in a large bowl of water at room temperature. Drain and thoroughly rinse the mushrooms, saving the mushroom liquid. Drain the liquid through cheesecloth and set aside. Chop the mushrooms into a larger dice than the onions. Simmer mushrooms with the onions, mushroom water, and lemon zest for 8-10 minutes. Drain and save half the cooking liquid. In a medium bowl, combine eggs, milk, sugar, currants, and rum and mix well. Add to the onion-mushroom mixture and the remaining cooking liquid. Pour into tart shells or greased ramekins, filling them 3/4 of the way. Place on baking sheet and bake 25-30 minutes until golden brown. *Serves 6.*

Jeffrey Allen

FRIED GREEN AND UGLY TOMATOES

The name comes from the **heirloom tomatoes** with which it is made, since they are irregularly shape, somewhat reminiscent of cabbage patch dolls. As a result, nobody seems to mind the somewhat unappetizing name.

1/2 cup balsamic vinegar
1/4 cup honey
2 green tomatoes
2 red tomatoes
Flour to coat
1 egg, beaten with a little water
1 cup panko or bread crumbs
2 egg-size ball fresh mozzarella
1 cup frying oil

Fresh basil, chiffonade
Extra virgin olive oil
Sea salt and pepper to taste

In a small saucepan, heat the balsamic vinegar and honey until it thickens into a syrup; let cool and set aside.

Cut the green tomatoes into ½-inch thick slices, and bread them, first dipping them in the flour, then in the egg wash, and finally in the bread crumbs; heat frying oil in a skillet until hot. Place these slices flat on the bottom of the skillet and fry them until done, about 3-4 minutes.

Slice the red tomatoes and the mozzarella cheese.

To serve, layer 2 slices of red tomatoes, 2 slices of fried green tomatoes, 2 slices of fresh mozzarella, and drizzle the balsamic and honey reduction, olive oil. Garnish with the basil chiffonade, sprinkle with salt and pepper. *Serves 4.*

ROMAINE SALAD WITH GORGONZOLA

This salad is very **easy to prepare** as well as delicious. Better yet, it can be put together in just a few minutes.

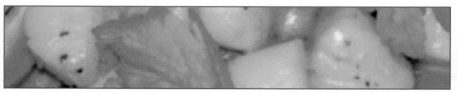

1 1/2 heads romaine lettuce, rinsed and dried
1 lb. Gorgonzola, crumbled
3/4 cup of house dressing (see house salad recipe)
1/2 lb. Toasted walnuts

Wash and dry the lettuce and de-vein. In a food processor, blend together about 1 cup of the Gorgonzola with the dressing until creamy. Pour the dressing over the lettuce and toss. Serve the salad on individual plates; sprinkle the toasted walnuts and remaining crumbled Gorgonzola. *Serves 5-6*

NANTUCKET'S FAMOUS BAY SCALLOPS

Nantucket's bay scallops, perhaps the **best-tasting** in the world, which is why they are among the most expensive.

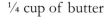

¼ cup of butter
1 tbsp. fresh lemon juice
1 tsp. finely chopped chives
1 lb. Nantucket bay scallops (if frozen, thaw and soak in a cup of milk for 30 minutes)
Sea salt and white pepper to taste

Drain and pat dry scallops. In a large skillet over low heat, melt the butter; add chives, and lemon juice. Bring to a simmer and add scallops. Sauté on all sides for 3-4 minutes over medium heat until opaque. Add sea salt and white pepper to taste. Serve on small appetizer plates. *Serves 4.*

Ann Rich

Jeffrey Allen

ROASTED BABY BEET SALAD

Great taste accompanies great color with these beets.

6 to 8 baby beets, rinsed clean and patted dry
Extra virgin olive oil
Sea salt and pepper to taste
1 small log goat cheese, crumbled
1 bunch chives

Preheat oven to 350 F.

Place beets in a deep baking pan. Drizzle with olive oil, sprinkle with salt and pepper, mixing well. Cover with aluminum foil and bake for about 1 hour, or until cook through. Allow to cool, and then cut each beet into quarters lengthwise.

To serve, place about 7 beet quarters to a portion. Top with crumbled goat cheese and sprinkle with chiffonade chives. Season with salt and pepper to taste. *Serves 4.*

ASPARAGUS APPETIZER

In Europe, asparagus is so prized that their appearance is **celebrated** as a harbinger of spring.

3 tbsp. red onions, minced
3 tbsp. scallions, minced
2 tbsp. butter, margarine or oil
1/2 cup uncooked yellow rice
Vegetable or chicken stock
1 lb. asparagus spears
1/4 cup crushed walnuts
1/4 cup white raisins, coarsely chopped
Parmesan cheese
Bread crumbs

In a large skillet, sauté the onions and scallions in the oil, margarine or butter. Stir in the yellow rice with enough vegetable or chicken stock to cover; stir slowly, but continually for 20 minutes. In a saucepan, boil or steam the asparagus al dente. Cover a large round platter with the rice mixture. Arrange the asparagus spears like spokes of a wheel on top of the rice. Top with crushed walnuts and white raisins. Finish with a sprinkling of Parmesan and bread crumbs. *Serves 6.*

CROSTINI OF SMOKED SALMON

All appetizers aren't complicated. Some are just **straightforward** and delicious, and this one is a case in point.

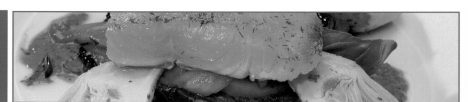

1/2 cup of smoked salmon, thinly sliced
6 tbsp. of unsalted butter
1/4 cup of finely grated Parmesan cheese
2 tbsp. of freshly chopped dill
1 tsp of fresh lime juice
10 slices of freshly baked bread, lightly toasted and cut into 1/4-inch-thick pieces
1/2 lb. oz. capers, drained and dried

In a food processor blend salmon, butter and cheese into a fine consistency. Spread a thin layer of this mixture over each piece of bread. Garnish each crostini with capers and a drop of fresh lime juice. *Serves 5.*

Ann Rich

ENDIVE AND PEAR SALAD

This **great combination** blends the sweetness of the pear, the salty creaminess of the Gorgonzola, the tartness of the endives and the crunchiness of the walnuts to make a wonderful mix of tastes and textures.

For the vinaigrette:
Champagne vinegar
Olive oil
1 shallot, finely diced
Sea salt and pepper

For the pears:
6 yellow endives
2 Bartlett pears
1/2cup Gorgonzola dolce cheese
1/2 cup toasted walnuts

For the vinaigrette, combine and mix well the vinegar, oil, shallot, salt and pepper. Set aside.

Slice the endives and the pears. Dress with the vinaigrette; season to taste with salt and pepper in a serving plate; top with crumbled gorgonzola. Garnish with the toasted walnuts. *Serves 4.*

GREEN VEGETABLE SALAD WITH CELERY PUREE

This wonderful salad tastes like a **summer garden**.

De Marco
RESTAURANT

For the salad:
3 leeks, tops removed,
split lengthwise, rinsed
and chopped
6 scallions, cleaned
and left whole
1/2 cup shelled fava
beans
1/2 cup fiddlehead
ferns, cleaned
1 bunch celery,
chopped
1 small white onion,
diced
2 cloves garlic, sliced
thin
1 cup vegetable stock

For the dressing:
Olive oil as needed
1/4 cup lemon juice

Blanch the leeks, scallions, fiddleheads, and fava beans in a large amount of boiling salted water for 1 minute; remove and plunge into ice water. (Vegetables should be bright green.).

In a small sauce pan sweat onions, celery and garlic in a little oil until celery is half-cooked. Add vegetable stock. Over medium heat, simmer until celery is soft. Place mixture into a blender, and slowly add a little olive oil, salt and pepper. Remove and allow mixture to come to room temperature.

In a sauté pan, reheat vegetables in a little oil; season with salt and pepper. Make a circle with the blanched leeks, scallions, fiddlehead ferns and fava beans on the bottom of a serving plate. Add celery puree in the center and top with hot vegetables. Serve with fresh lemon slices and a side of extra virgin olive oil dressing and toasted thin crostini. *Serves 4.*

Jeffrey Allen

NANTUCKET CLAM CHOWDER

From the days of Moby Dick to the present, this is a **longtime favorite**.

6 tbsp. of butter
3/4 lb. thick-cut pancetta or slab bacon, cut into 1/4-inch dice
2 celery stalks, finely chopped
1 parsnip, finely chopped
1 yellow onion, finely chopped
1/2 cups of all-purpose flour
1 lb. of Russert (or Yukon Gold) potatoes, cut into ½-inch dice
16 Little Neck clams, thoroughly cleaned
2 cups of clam juice
1 cup of light cream
2 tbsp. of chopped mint
2 tbsp. of chopped flat-leaf parsley
1 tbsp of chopped thyme
Sea salt and coarse ground black pepper to taste

In a large pot, add butter and crisp bacon or pancetta for 4-5 minutes. Add chopped celery, parsnip and onion, and cook for 2-3 minutes. Add flour and stir constantly to keep the mixture smooth. Cook for 2-3 minutes.

Over medium heat, add clam juice. Allow the chowder to reduce 3-4 minutes, while continually stirring to keep a smooth consistency. If lumps develop, use a whisk. Stir in potatoes and simmer for about 12-15 min. Stir in the cream, mint, parsley, thyme, sea salt and pepper, and let simmer for another 5-10 minutes. Finally, add clams and cook until shells open. Serve with clams propped up in a circle in each bowl. *Serves 6 to 8.*

NO-OIL SALAD DRESSING

For those who wish to limit their intake of any kind of fats, including olive oil, here is the **perfect salad dressing** that combines sweet and tart to great effect.

1/2 cup orange juice
1/4 cup white vinegar
1/4 cup currents, chopped
2 tbsp. cilantro, finely minced
1 tsp. fresh lime zest
1 tsp. ground fennel seeds

In a bowl, whisk together all the ingredients until thoroughly blended and toss with salad greens, garnished as desired. Season to taste. Yield: about 2 cups.

HOUSE SALAD

No house worth its sea salt should be without a **signature salad**. This one is ours, resplendent of summer with a variety of lettuces and a zesty dressing that provides a refreshing tang.

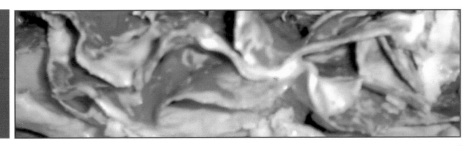

For the salad:
1 1/2 heads of mixed lettuces (Boston, red leaf, romaine, watercress, etc.)

For the dressing:
4 tbsp. peanut oil
3 1/2 tbsp. olive oil
2 1/2 tbsp. champagne vinegar
1 tsp. Dijon mustard
1/2 clove garlic, finely minced
Sea salt and pepper to taste
Parmesan shavings for garnish

For the salad dressing, mix all the ingredients and whisk together. Refrigerate. When ready to serve, rinse and dry well lettuce leaves to rid of excess moisture; add dressing. Garnish with a few shaved slices of Parmesan cheese. *Serves 5-6.*

HOT MACARONI SALAD

Everyone thinks of macaroni salad as being a dish served cold. But this one is **served hot**, and it's just as delicious.

DeMarco
RESTAURANT

1/2 lb. elbow macaroni or small shells, cooked
1/4 cup celery, chopped
1/2 red onion, finely chopped
1/4 cup of extra virgin olive oil
1/2 pound of cream cheese or a low fat substitute
1 tsp of red pepper flakes
Chicken or vegetable broth (as needed to moisten), about 1 cup
1/4 cup flat-leaf parsley

Boil and drain the macaroni according to the package directions. In a large saucepan over high heat, add all the ingredients and stir until thoroughly heated. Reserve ½ cup of the cooking liquid and pour over the dish.

HEIRLOOM TOMATO SUMMER SALAD

These tomatoes really taste the way tomatoes should, **naturally vine-ripened**, the way we remember as children when they came straight from the **garden** and before the days of picking unripe fruit and "gassing" them artificially to make them bright red in the trucks that transported them to supermarkets.

2 red heirloom tomatoes, cut in ½-inch-thick slices
2 green zebra heirloom tomatoes, cut into 1.2-inch-thick slices
2 egg-size balls of fresh buffalo mozzarella cheese, cut into ½-inch-thick slices
Fresh basil
Extra virgin olive oil
Sea salt and pepper

On a serving plate, arrange the tomatoes and mozzarella in alternating slices: one slice of red tomato, one slice of green tomato and one slice of cheese. Repeat for each portion. Drizzle with olive oil, sprinkle with salt and pepper to taste. Garnish with basil leaves. *Serves 4.*

SEA SCALLOP SALAD

An easily prepared and **versatile dish**, this salad can be served as an appetizer/salad or even as a main dish, the only difference being the size of the portion. Serve on a seasoned bed of sautéed mushrooms and wilted spinach.

1 lb. sea scallops
3 tbsp. olive oil
Paprika
Coarsely ground black pepper
Sea salt to taste

In a large pan, sauté the sea scallops in the olive oil, the paprika and coarsely ground black pepper until scallops turn opaque, about 3-4 minutes. Present on a bed of lettuce leaves. *Serves 4.*

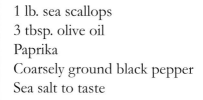

ANGEL HAIR (CAPELLINI) PASTA WITH SHRIMP*

We estimate that **100,000 people** have ordered this dish in our 28-year history. In a faithful ritual, guests order this meal as necessary to the spirit of their Nantucket holiday.

For the sauce:
1/3 cup olive oil
4 tbsp. garlic, minced
2 anchovies, diced
1 tsp. red pepper flakes
1/4 cup white wine
2 qts. tomatoes, chopped
1 tbsp. thyme, minced
1 tbsp. oregano, minced
2 tbsp. balsamic vinegar
1 lb. shrimp (preferably size #20), cleaned and veins removed
1 lb. angel hair pasta, cooked al dente and thoroughly drained

In a large sauté pan, heat up the olive oil. Add the garlic, herbs, red pepper flakes and anchovies. Cook until fragrant or about 6-8 minutes. Add the wine. Cook for an additional 5 minutes. Add the tomatoes, and reduce heat to a simmer for about 1 1/2 hours. Turn off heat. Add the balsamic vinegar, salt and pepper to taste. Sauté the shrimp in a separate large sauté pan over medium to high heat with a little olive oil. When pink, turn over shrimp so as to cook both sides evenly, about 2-3 minutes. Add the sauce to the shrimp along with the drained angel hair pasta. Cook for 1-2 minutes, stirring the pasta until thoroughly coated with the sauce. *Serves 6.*

CHESTNUT PAPPARDELLE WITH SCALLION PESTO SAUCE

Perhaps it's the **chestnuts** that make this excellent pasta dish especially warming on a cool fall evening..

DeMarco
RESTAURANT

For the pasta:
2 tbsp. chestnut purée
1/2 cup chestnut flour
2 cups all-purpose flour
1/2 tsp. salt
Dash of nutmeg and black pepper
2 tbsp. warm water
2 tbsp. olive oil
2 eggs, beaten

For the pesto:
2 cups fresh basil leaves
1/2 cup chopped scallions
1/4 cup pine nuts
2 cloves garlic
3/4 cup parmesan cheese
3/4 cup extra virgin olive oil
2 cups fresh snap peas
Sea salt and white pepper to taste

In a large bowl, combine all dry pasta ingredients. In a second bowl, combine all wet pasta ingredients. Make a well in the middle of the dry ingredients and put all wet ingredients in the well. Slowly incorporate the wet and dry ingredients until a dough forms. Knead for ten minutes, adjusting with water and flour to achieve a non-sticky, elastic dough. Let rest for half an hour. On a large lightly floured surface, roll out the dough until it is almost translucent. Cut into 1-inch wide "ribbons". Sprinkle ribbons with flour and set aside. The irregular pasta remains, left at the edges of the uniformly cut pasta, is where the Badly Cut gets its name.

In a food processor, place the basil, scallions, pine nuts and garlic with 1/3 of the olive oil. Turn on processor to medium speed and slowly blend in the remainder of the olive oil. Remove and stir in the parmesan cheese. Season with salt and pepper.

Meanwhile, in a large pot, bring salted water to rolling boil. Stir in pasta ribbons and cook for 1 minute. Add the snap peas. Continue cooking for another 2-3 minutes; remove pasta and peas; place in a large serving bowl. Spoon pesto over hot pasta and toss thoroughly. Serve hot. *Serves 6.*

Jeffrey Allen

SHRIMP-STUFFED JUMBO PASTA SHELLS

Pasta shells stuffed with shrimp look like a **sea animal**. When customers would see this dish being served at a nearby table they would ask, "What's that?!" This happened so often that it became **humorously** called by the staff and ordered in kitchen jargon as the "What's that? dish."

1 lb. jumbo pasta shells, barely cooked and drained
1 lb. shrimp, peeled and veins removed

For the stuffing:
1 lb. ricotta cheese
1 egg
1/4 cup fresh mint, finely chopped
1/4 cup fresh parsley
1/3 cup chopped walnuts, minced
1/2 tsp. black pepper
1/2 tsp. nutmeg
1 tsp. sea salt

Basic tomato sauce (see recipe p. 80)

Boil the pasta shells to 3/4 of the cooking time indicated on the package (about 7 or 8 minutes). Drain and set aside. Parboil shrimp and set aside. In a large bowl, mix the cheese, egg, mint, parsley, pepper, nutmeg and salt. Coat the bottom of a baking dish with a 1/2 inch of basic tomato sauce .Using a teaspoon, fill the pasta shell with the cheese mixture. Stuff a shrimp headfirst into one end, allowing the tail to protrude outside the pasta shell. Place the stuffed pasta into a baking dish with the tomato sauce. Repeat the process until all the shells have been stuffed. Cover with aluminum foil and bake in a 350-degree oven for 30 minutes. *Serves 6.*

Note: For a decorative effect, add a stripe of green pesto sauce across each shell.

LINGUINE WITH LOBSTER TAILS AND CLAMS

This dish is an **Italian classic**, perfect during the summer with a glass of chardonnay. Serve it with fresh bread to soak up the sauce.

DeMarco
RESTAURANT

20 cherry stone clams
4 cloves garlic, minced
1 cup olive oil
2 lobster tails

2 cups dry white wine
20 Little Neck clams
20 mussels
1/2 cup of parsley, chopped
Linguine, enough for 4 people

Steam the chowder clams in a large sieve over 1 quart boiling water, until they are just open. Do not overcook. Reserve the cooking liquid. Chop the clams and set them aside in their own liquid. In a large saucepan, sauté the minced garlic in the olive oil for about 5 minutes. Steam the lobster tails until they turn red. Over low heat, ad the Little Neck clams and white wine to the sautéed garlic. Steam for about 5 minutes. When they open, add the mussels and steam for an additional 2 minutes or until the mussels open. Add the chopped clams. Cut each lobster tail into 6 pieces and add to the sauce (you may remove the shell or leave it on).

Cook the pasta in salted boiling water for 7 minutes, or according to package directions.

With a slotted spoon, separate the chopped clams from the broth. Strain the broth and toss with the pasta. Top each serving with the chopped cherry stone clams, the Little Necks, the mussels in their shells, and the lobster tails. Garnish with freshly chopped parsley. *Serves 4-6 people.*

LOBSTER CANNELLONI

Another classic, this dish is among the **most requested** on the DeMarco menu.

For the filling:
1/4 lb. butter
1/2 cup all-purpose flour
1/2 qt. whole milk
5 ears fresh corn kernels, cut off the cob
2 (1 1/4 - 1 1/2 lbs.) whole lobsters, boiled, cleaned and diced into ½-inch pieces

1/2 cup chopped basil

For the pasta:
1 1/4 cups all-purpose flour or pasta flour
3 large eggs, lightly beaten
1 tsp. sea salt
Preheat oven to 400 degrees.

In a medium saucepan, melt butter. Add flour and stir to form a paste; cook for 6 minutes. Whisk in milk. Add corn kernels and cook until sauce thickens, about 10 minutes. Remove from heat and set aside to cool. Stir in lobster meat and parsley; reserve

Prepare the pasta. In a large bowl, place the flour and make a well in the center; add eggs and salt, and with a fork, slowly incorporate, whisking in the ingredients. Once the dough ball is formed, knead for 8-10 min until dough is smooth and shiny. Cover with plastic wrap and let rest for 30 minutes or overnight in refrigerator. Remove from the refrigerator; allow dough to come to room temperature. Roll out 1/8-inch thick sheets on a lightly floured surface. Cut dough into 4-inch to 6-inch medium-size rectangles and set aside.

Place a small amount of filling on a rectangle of pasta; carefully roll it up in the shape of a fat cigar, making sure no filling protrudes from the ends. Repeat until all the pasta rectangles have been stuffed, saving some filling to top the pasta.

Place cannelloni into a baking dish and top with a generous portion of the lobster filling. Bake in preheated oven until hot, bubbly and slightly browned on top. Sprinkle liberally with fresh basil and serve hot. Plate 3 cannelloni per serving. *Serves 4.*

QUICK PASTA WITH RICOTTA

Pasta coupled with ricotta is one of the **most traditional** pairings in Italian cookery.

1/2 lb. partially cooked pasta (penne or bowtie)
3/4 cup water
1/4 cup of butter or butter substitute
1/4 cup red onion, minced
1 cup low-fat ricotta cheese
1/4 cup fresh thyme
Coarsely ground black pepper, to taste
1/4 cup of extra virgin olive oil (optional)

In a large pot, place the half-cooked drained pasta with ¾ cup of the cooking water. Add the butter or butter substitute, onions, ricotta cheese, and thyme. Cover pot and cook over low heat for 5 minutes. Uncover and stir continually for an additional 4-5 minutes. *Serves 4.*

Jeffrey Allen

LINGUINE WITH CLAMS

Another **all-time favorite**, especially when the clams are super-fresh.

For the pasta:
1 package dry linguine
Sea salt

For the sauce and clams:

2 tbsp. minced shallots
1 tbsp. thinly sliced garlic
Olive oil for cooking and finishing
2 lbs. fresh clams, rinsed and scrubbed
1 cup dry white wine
1/2 tsp red pepper flakes
1/4 cup chopped parsley

In a large pot of boiling, salted water, place pasta, stirring occasionally. In a sauté pan, sweat garlic and shallots in a little oil. Add clams, then white wine, and red pepper flakes. Reduce heat and cover; steam until clams open. Stir in pasta and toss in pan for at least one minute. Remove from heat. Add 2 tbsp. olive oil and sprinkle with parsley. *Serves 4.*

RISOTTO WITH BABY PEAS AND PISTACHIO NUTS

Rice when **masterfully handled**, in an infinite variety of risottos, comes close to replacing pasta in the Italian regions of Piedmont, Venetia and Lombardy. One such magnificent recipe is this one.

DeMarco
R E S T A U R A N T

For the ingredients:
2 tbsp. butter
1 tbsp. olive oil
2 large garlic cloves [pressed]
1 cup arborio rice
1 cup dry white wine
4 cups chicken stock, heated to simmering
1 cup fresh baby peas
1/2 cup grated Parmesan cheese
Sea salt, and freshly ground pepper
½ cup whole pistachio nuts

In a large skillet, melt the butter in the olive oil over medium heat. Add garlic and sauté; do not brown. Add rice and stock, a ladle at a time and continue to stir slowly and continually until all the liquid had been absorbed and rice is coated. Taste throughout the cooking process. Cook about 40 minutes. Stir in the peas and continue to add the rest of the stock, ½ cup at a time. Taste again after 5 minutes; the rice should be just tender to the bite. Add white wine to the rice mixture until the liquid has been absorbed. Remove from heat, gradually stir in the cheese, and season with the salt and pepper to taste. Mound the risotto into a warmed, shallow bowls, and garnish with pistachio nuts. *Serves 4*

Jeffrey Allen

LINGUINE PRIMAVERA CON FRUTTA DI MARE

Serve this **mouth-watering** pasta primavera in large bowls and sprinkle liberally with freshly chopped parsley. For a beautifully presented dish, place the fish, scallops and shrimp on the top of the pasta where they will be clearly visible!

2 (5-oz.) firm, white-fleshed fish fillets
1 lb. bay scallops
1 lb. medium-size shrimp
8 tbsp. butter
3 onions, minced
3 carrots, julienned
2 cups light cream
1 1/2. (16-oz) packages linguine
3 zucchini, julienned
1 (10-oz. package) frozen peas, defrosted
or 1 (15-oz. can) cooked peas
1 lb. asparagus spears, scraped, blanched
and cut into 2-inch pieces
3 cucumbers, julienned
3 oz. Parmesan cheese, grated
Sea salt and pepper to taste
¼ cup chopped parsley for garnish

Pat dry the fish and scallops; clean and devein the shrimp. In a large skillet, sauté onions and carrots in 5 tablespoons of butter over medium heat until soft, about 10 minutes.
Meanwhile, cook linguine in salted boiling water for about 7 minutes. Drain and rinse in cold water.

Pour cream over onion/carrot mixture; bring to a boil. Add zucchini, peas, and asparagus, stirring consistently. Add the fish, scallops, shrimp and cucumbers. Cook for about 2 minutes. Add parmesan and season with salt and pepper. Toss the linguine in the sauce and add remaining butter. *Serves 8.*

QUICK AND EASY BROILED FRESH TOMATO SAUCE

If you think of pasta sauces as a **time-consuming** affair involving hours of slow simmering and a lot of stirring, think again. This is the easiest, quickest, thin sauce you will ever make—and it doesn't even require a saucepan, never mind a wooden spoon.

6 large tomatoes, sliced thin
fresh basil leaves
tuna, anchovies, cooked chicken or bacon
Sea salt and freshly ground pepper to taste

On a flat, lightly greased baking sheet, place the tomato slices. Place a basil leaf and parsley on each slice. Cover each one with selected topping(s). Broil for 5 minutes, making sure that the tomatoes do not burn. Season with sea salt and pepper. Scoop onto cooked pasta or rice.

STUFFED CALAMARATA PASTA RING

A uniquely festive and versatile dish.

For the pasta water:
1/2 lb. calamarata
1 qt. salted water and 2 qts. Chicken or veal stock
1/4 cup chopped thyme
1 tbsp. honey
1 tbsp. fresh lemon juice
4 cloves garlic, chopped
1/4 cup scallions, chopped
1 tbsp. fennel seeds
2 tbsp. whole cloves
Sea salt and white pepper to taste

Calamarata has been made for the past 300 years and originates in the town of Gragnano, Italy, named after its wonderful grana wheat. This festive-looking pasta dish is sauceless and is served cool or at room temperature. The advantage of this elaborate appetizer/entrée is that the individual "rings" can be filled with leftover ingredients in your refrigerator. In the picture above, we have painted the plate with an olive oil infused basil and chive sauce (in a food processor, simply blend ½ cup olive oil and 8 oz. of basil and 6 oz. of chive). In the photo,, the fillings shown right to left are as follows: cold soft-shelled crab with red caviar; steamed asparagus and halved green olives; red caviar and pickled eggplant; sesame seared tuna; mushroom with a potato crisp; pickled pearl onions; black caviar; grilled red pepper with slightly charred orange zest; marinated small green olives and red caviar; fresh seasoned tuna with string beans and (center) braised cabbage. The trick here, however, is to have all the fillings prepared and handy to begin stuffing the individual pasta rounds as soon as they are cool enough to handle, since this pasta's opening is prone to close if it is not promptly filled, a situation that demands fast work. The flavors and seasonings added to the cooking water create a unique taste to the pasta itself.

In a large pot, place all the ingredients and bring to a boil for 5 minutes, then add the pasta. Cook the pasta slightly past the traditional al dente point and just before the noodle will start to crack (observe carefully). Drain in cold water and place on a flat sheet, open-side up. Begin to insert the desired filling as soon as the individual pieces are cooled. Place the filled rings in a circle on a large serving plate. *Serves 4.*

STUFFED CALAMARATA PASTA RING

Jeffrey Allen

BASIC TOMATO SAUCE

For a **beginner**, tomato sauce is the best recipe to practice on, precisely because it is so versatile

This recipe is the basic foundation of any tomato sauce, open to additions, experimentation and changes. Adding mushrooms or bell peppers will make it heartier; adding red pepper flakes or a pinch of cayenne pepper for a spicier treat with a little heat. Dry white wine can be substituted for the red wine, especially if the sauce is served with seafood. For a beginner, tomato sauce is the best recipe to practice on, precisely because it is so versatile and can be adapted to any cooking style and taste. Just go with your creativity! Enjoy!

For the ingredients:
1 onion, finely chopped
1/2 cup extra virgin olive oil

½ cup good dry red wine
6 garlic cloves, minced

1 carrot, finely chopped
2 stalks celery, finely chopped

6 pounds vine-ripened tomatoes
2 bay leaves
1 bunch of basil, chopped (leaves only)
½ cup parsley, chopped

Sea salt and pepper to taste

In a large saucepan, sauté onion in ½ the olive oil for about 10 minutes. Add the wine and garlic and cook over medium heat until liquid is reduced. Add the rest of the olive oil and carrots and celery. Sauté until fragrant and the onions are translucent, stirring often. Add the tomatoes, bay leaf, parsley and basil and stir. Simmer on medium heat for 1-2 hours, stirring occasionally. Salt and pepper to taste. *Serves 6.*

CREAMLESS CREAM SAUCE

It is a very good **accompaniment** to pasta shapes, such as orchiette.

This sauce is made especially for the calorie-and cholesterol-conscious, but who nevertheless still love creamy sauces. This recipe will allay any fears—nary a dairy product in sight. It is a very good accompaniment to pasta shapes, such as orchiette. This sauce is also good with fish.

For the sauce:
4 lbs. tomatoes, coarsely chopped
2 lbs. red and yellow bell peppers, cored, seeded and quartered
1 lb. Vidalia onions, coarsely chopped
1 tsp. mint leaves, minced
2 medium avocados
1/4 cup olive oil
Sea salt and pepper to taste

For the pasta:
1 lb. orchiette cooked al dente and drained
Grated Parmesan cheese (optional)

In a large pot, combine the tomatoes, bell peppers and onions, and bring to a boil over high heat. Reduce heat and allow to simmer for 30 minutes, add salt and pepper, mint and honey; set aside to cool.

With a spoon, scoop out the flesh from the avocados; place in a bowl and add olive oil. Once the tomato mixture is cool, place all the ingredients in a food processor until completely blended. Return to the pot over low heat and cook for 15 minutes. Drain the cooked pasta thoroughly and return it to the same pot on low heat, add two cups of sauce and stir and simmer for 2 to 3 minutes. Serve on a shallow platter with a separate bowl of sauce. Sprinkle with grated Parmesan, if desired.

PASTA IN CHOCOLATE SAUCE

If you ever serve this recipe, you will see your friends' faces change from downright **skepticism** to surprise and delight.

DeMarco
RESTAURANT

When chocolate came to Italy from the New World, the Italians put it into everything. Eventually It even found its way into their pastas. Although the idea is startling to most people today, it was an established traditional dish of my grandparents' generation. The hint of melted chocolate in the sauce and the small amount of unsweetened cocoa powder in the freshly made pasta results in an unexpectedly deep flavor; it truly offers a new and different experience on the palate. If you ever serve this recipe, you will see your friends' faces change from downright skepticism to surprise and delight.

For the sauce:
1/2 cup extra virgin olive oil
1 large garlic clove, finely chopped
4 ounces pancetta, finely chopped
1/2 cup of scallions, finely chopped with a portion of the green stems included
1 large celery stalk, finely chopped
1 medium carrot, finely chopped
1/2 bunch of mint, finely chopped
1/2 bunch of flat leaf parsley, finely chopped
1 lb of lean ground veal
1 cup of good, dry red wine
2 cups of canned whole tomatoes
2 tbsp. of balsamic vinegar
3 tbsp. of white raisins, chopped
4 tbsp. of chopped walnuts
2 tbsp of semi-sweet chocolate chips
1 tbsp. of granulated sugar
1 tbsp. ground fennel seeds
Sea salt and black pepper to taste

For the pasta (tagliatelle):
3 cups of all purpose flour
3 extra large eggs
1 tbsp. olive oil
1/2 tsp. of salt
5 tbsp. of unsweetened cocoa powder

Place flour in the center of a large working surface, preferably wood. Make a well with a fork, large enough to fit the eggs, olive oil, salt and cocoa powder. Begin to work the eggs and flour together with your fork, slowly incorporating the sides of the well. Knead by hand until the dough forms a smooth texture and an even color all around. Do not overknead. Set aside for ½ hour.

Cut dough into pieces the size of lemons, flattening them with your hand to a ¼-inch thick; put them through the widest setting on your pasta maker. Fold dough back onto itself and put it through again. Move the setting down a notch at each pass, finishing at the second-to-last thickness on your pasta maker.

Meanwhile, heat the oil, adding chopped ingredients and pancetta. Sauté over low heat for about 10-12 minutes. Add ground veal and blend into the sautéed ingredients, stirring slowly. Add the wine and continue to sauté for 5 minutes. Add the tomatoes, and season with sea salt and black pepper. Simmer slowly for about 30-35 minutes.

In a small bowl, whisk together the balsamic vinegar, white raisins, walnuts, ground fennel, chocolate chips and sugar in a small bowl, and set aside. When the sauce has reduced, add this mixture and slowly stir all the ingredients together for another 10-12 minutes. *Serves 8*

Serve in a large dish, generously pouring the sauce on top.

RISOTTO CLASSICO WITH SAFFRON

But rice, along with **potatoes and pasta**, is one of the must-have staples in the world's larder.

2 pinches saffron
1/4 cup warm milk
1 tsp peppercorns, roasted and coarsely crushed
6 tbsp. butter
1 large onion, chopped
1 cup arborio rice
4 cups vegetable stock [chicken, beef, or seafood]
Salt and pepper to taste
1 cup grated Parmesan cheese

Many people do not equate rice as a typical Italian ingredient. But rice, along with potatoes and pasta, is one of the must-have staples in the world's larder. It also has a way of representing a country via a national dish: Spain has its saffron-scented, tumeric- tinted paella, Indonesia has its very elaborate rijstafel, India has its spice-laden curry, Turkey has its raison-dotted pilaf, and Italy has its rich and creamy risotto that pays homage to a very special and very Italian rice—arborio.

Soak saffron strands in the warm milk. Roast and crush the peppercorns. In a saucepan, heat butter; add onion. Sauté over medium flame for 2 minute. Add rice and sauté for 6-8 minutes. Add a ladle of the stock along with saffron liquid, salt and pepper. Reduce heat and stir constantly over low heat until the stock is absorbed. Incorporate the remaining stock a little at a time, allowing it to be absorbed by the rice mixture before adding more. When all the stock has been thoroughly absorbed, the rice should be cooked and the risotto should be moist and creamy. Gently fold in half the grated cheese. Garnish the completed dish with the remaining grated cheese. *Serves 6.*

CANNELLONI DI CASA

When it comes to **Old World Italian** cookery, it doesn't come much more classical than this dish.

For the pasta:
1 lb. fresh pasta (cannelloni) See standard pasta recipe, p. 21

For the filling:
1 lb. mortadella, chopped
8-12 oz. (1 1/2 8-oz. packages) soften cream cheese
3 eggs
1 cup ricotta cheese
1/4 cup chopped parsley
1 tsp nutmeg
1/2 cup grated pecorino
1 lb. fresh spinach, stems removed
Sea salt and pepper to taste

For the sauce:
1/2 cup tomato puree
1/4 lb. butter
1 1/2 cups light cream
1/2 cup grated pecorino

Preheat oven to 350 degrees.

Cut fresh pasta into 6 inch squares. Cook pasta in salted boiling water for 5 minutes, drain and place the pasta in cold water.

In a large bowl, combine all the ingredients, next blanch the spinach, drain and set aside to cool. Squeeze the spinach dry, chop coarsely and stir spinach in with the filling mixture.

Place a teaspoon of the filling in the center of each pasta square and roll until the filling is distributed. Place the rolls on a large buttered baking dish. Pour the sauce over the cannelloni and sprinkle with pecorino. Bake in preheated oven at 350 degrees for 20 minutes. *Serves 6-8.*

OLD WORLD SUNDAY SPAGHETTI SAUCE

We have served this festive sauce with meatballs at the DeMarco restaurant once every season for **28 years**. Served preferable over a flat pasta and sprinkled with cheese (optional) along with a favorite meat dish, or seafood and a green salad, this makes a hearty and heart-warming meal.

1/2 cup good red wine
1/2 lb. beef or pork shoulder
1/3 cup extra virgin olive oil
4 cloves of garlic, minced
1/4 cup carrots, finely chopped
1/4 cup celery, finely chopped
1/4 cup bell pepper, finely chopped
1 tbsp. ground fennel
1 tbsp. dried parsley
1 tbsp. dried basil
2 tbsp. balsamic vinegar
1 bunch fresh parsley, coarsely chop
1 bunch fresh basil, coarsely chopped
2 (6-oz) cans tomato paste
1 (16-oz) can tomato purée
4 (28-oz.) cans whole tomatoes in sauce, mashed
1 tsp. red pepper flakes
Sea salt & pepper to taste
1 lb. flat pasta

In a large pot, heat olive oil over medium heat. Add meat and brown well on both sides. Remove and set aside for another day.

Reduce heat to a low flame and stir tomato paste and dry ingredients into the same pot. Cook for 12-14 minutes, stirring slowly and continuously until the paste turns a darker color. Place in a bowl and set aside.

In the same pot over low heat, add three tablespoons of olive oil and the garlic, onion, carrots, celery and bell peppers. Sauté and stir slowly for 8-10 minutes.

To this mixture, add tomato puree and whole tomatoes. Bring to a slow boil, then reduce heat and stir in balsamic vinegar, red pepper flakes and 1/2 cup good red wine. Cook for 45 minutes, stirring often. Next, stir in the cooked tomato paste and dry ingredient mixture. Simmer for 30 minutes, stirring occasionally. Serves a lot of people

"BADLY CUT" PASTA WITH BOSCAIOLA SAUCE

When you think the mushrooms are done, pour yourself a glass of wine and leave them in the oven for another 5 minutes!" This recipe yields sauce to spare for the next day.

5 lbs. mushrooms (assorted button mushrooms, portabella, and shitake)
1 cup olive oil
Salt and white pepper to taste
1/2 lb. sliced prosciutto, chopped
1 qt. light cream
2 1/2 lbs. vine-ripened tomatoes (chopped)
1/2 tbsp. fresh sage leaves, julienned and chopped
1/2 lb. Parmesan cheese rinds

For the garnish:
Parmesan cheese shavings

Preheat oven to 450 degrees.

Simply the best—better than all the rest--this rich and creamy sauce is a signature creation for us and has been on our menu for decades. Patrons have said that they come to Nantucket for this recipe alone, and many customers end up begging for it on their way out. Don't be dismayed by the amount of light cream in the sauce. Once you taste it, you'll fell that it is well worth cheating on your diet! The secret to this sauce is the oven-roasted mushrooms and long, slow cooking. Be sure to leave them in the oven until they are deep brown and dry. Like our chef says, "When you think the mushrooms are done, pour yourself a glass of wine and leave them in the oven for another 5 minutes!" This recipe yields sauce to spare for the next day. As for the pasta, the name hails from a time before machines when the cooks would use the scraps left over from pasta dough that had uneven or ragged edges.

Clean and dice mushrooms and coat in olive oil, salt and white pepper. Roast in the oven for 45 minutes, or until crispy. Set aside.

In a large saucepan, sauté prosciutto and half the sage until fragrant, about 5-7 minutes. Add the cream and bring to a boil, stirring often so the cream does not separate. Turn the heat down to medium-low. Add the chopped tomatoes, Parmesan cheese rinds and the roasted mushrooms. Lower heat and simmer; reduce sauce for three hours, adding the remaining sage just before removing sauce from heat.

Remove the cheese rinds before serving. Serve with fresh wide-ribbon pasta. Sprinkle fresh sage on the pasta and a few thin shavings of Parmesan to garnish. *Serves 10-12.*

Jeffrey Allen

PORTABELLA CRUSTED CHICKEN WITH SPINACH SAUCE

This dish combines **good taste and good health.** Firm white-fleshed fish, such as halibut, can be substituted for the chicken, if desired. The sauce can be prepared either ahead of time or while the chicken is baking.

DeMarco
RESTAURANT

For the chicken:
2 lbs portabella mushrooms, finely chopped
2 garlic cloves, finely chopped
2 shallots, chopped
4 tbsp. olive oil
6 large boneless chicken breasts
Season to taste

For the sauce:
8 cups chopped spinach.
1 medium yellow onion finely chopped
3 tbsp. of butter
1 cup chicken broth
1 tsp honey
1 tbsp white wine vinegar
Season to taste

In a large skillet, sauté mushrooms, shallots and garlic in 4 tablespoons of olive oil for about 8-10 minutes, or until soft. Place the mixture in a food processor to form a thick paste. Season the chicken breasts thoroughly with salt and pepper and cover each breast evenly with the blended mixture. Place each breast n a lightly greased baking dish. Cover the dish with aluminum foil. Bake for 30-35 minutes, in a 300 degree oven, until the chicken is cooked through and the drippings run clear.

Blanch the spinach in a large pot of boiling water. Drain the spinach and when cool squeeze the excess water out of the spinach by hand. In a large skillet, sauté the onion and butter until soft, add the chicken broth, white wine vinegar, garlic, honey and bring to a boil; stir continuously until reduced by half. Add the spinach and continue to cook for 2-3 minutes. Place the mixture in a food processor and blend until smooth.

Remove the aluminum foil from the baking dish and broil for 5 minutes. Place chicken breasts in the center of a large plate and ladle a generous portion of the sauce (be sure to reheat the sauce) over the chicken. *Serves 6.*

CUBED MONK FISH WITH ROASTED RHUBARB

This unusual combination features two very East Coast ingredients—**fresh fish and rhubarb.** The lobster-like texture of the monk fish goes particularly well with the piquant taste of the rhubarb.

DeMarco
RESTAURANT

For the rhubarb:
2 lbs. of rhubarb, cut into four-inch pieces
1/4 cup honey

For the fish:
2 lbs. of monk fish, cut into one-inch cubes
3 whole eggs
3/4 cup flour

For the garnish:
1 tbsp. cilantro
Fresh lime zest

Preheat oven to 350 degrees.

Parboil rhubarb with honey for 25-30 minutes. Set aside and allow to cool.

Meanwhile, beat the eggs until well blended. Brush the cubed monk fish with the egg wash. Dip the fish into flour, shaking off excess flour and bake for 8-10 minutes. Place a generous portion of the honeyed rhubarb in the center of the dinner plate. Top with the baked monk fish. *Serves 4.*

STUFFED BEEF ROLLS

This is great for **parties or cocktails** at formal dinners. These bite-size rolls of roast beef are perfect for eliminating the chore of negotiating big slabs of roast beef while providing the comfort-food aspect of the old-fashioned taste of the family Sunday dinner roast.

1 lb. eye round roast
1/2 lb. grated parmesan cheese
1/3 cup butter
1/4 cup olive oil
10 bay leaves
Season to taste

Place the roast in the freezer for 45 minutes to an hour. Using an electric knife, cut the meat into 1/8 inch slices. Pound the meat gently into thin rounds, be careful not to tear the pieces. In the center of each piece of meat place a teaspoon of butter, two teaspoons of parmesan cheese, and season to taste with salt and pepper. Roll each piece firmly and set them aside. In a large skillet place a ¼ cup of olive oil over medium heat and add the bay leaves. Next add the rolls (six to eight at a time) and sauté for 1 minute, be sure to brown on all sides. Remove the cooked beef rolls and repeat the process until all are cooked. Serve on a warm plate with small slices of fresh bread. *Serves 6.*

VEAL SCALLOPS IN A SPICY MUSHROOM SAUCE

Veal makes an excellent **vehicle for vegetables** with strong characteristics. In this case, it is the perfect foil for mushrooms, ripe tomatoes and Sicilian olives, making it a very tasty Italian dish.

1/2 cup pancetta, diced
6 tbsp. clarified butter
1 1/2 lbs. veal scallops
3/4 cup sliced red onion
1 cup sliced mushrooms
1 cup chopped tomatoes
1 cup pitted Sicilian olives
3/4 cup white wine
1/3 cup flour
1/4 fresh chopped parsley
Red pepper flakes according to taste
Season to taste

Pound and flatten the veal scallops, dust with flour, and season with salt and pepper. In a skillet, sauté the pancetta over medium heat in butter until browned, and place in a separate bowl. Sauté the veal in the same pan for 4-5 minutes, and place in a separate bowl.

In the same skillet, over medium heat place the browned pancetta, the white wine, red pepper flakes and flour, bring to a simmer and stir continuously to produce a smooth emulsion. Add the onions and continue to simmer for 10 minutes. Next, stir in the tomatoes, mushrooms and olives; reduce heat and simmer for 15 minutes, now place the veal scallops in the skillet and simmer for an additional 8-10 minutes.

Place the scallops on serving plates and cover with pan sauce and garnish with chopped parsley. *Serves 4-6 people.*

RACK OF LAMB WITH HERBED PESTO SAUCE

A favorite for Easter in Mediterranean countries and much of Europe, the **dramatic presentation** of this dish makes for a festive occasion no matter when it is served.

DeMarco
RESTAURANT

For the lamb:
1 rack of Colorado lamb (8 ribs)
1 tbsp. rosemary
3 tbsp. olive oil
1 tsp. of black pepper
1 tsp. of salt

For the pesto sauce:
1/4 cup of minced parsley
1/4 cup of minced mint
1/4 cup of minced basil
1/4 cup of olive oil
1 minced anchovy
1 tbsp. of minced garlic

Bring lamb to room temperature. Whisk together rosemary, pepper, salt and olive oil; set aside for 30 minutes. Brush the entire rack with the marinade. Grill for a total of 6 minutes per side, turning the chops over twice.

In a food processor, blend the herbs, anchovy, garlic and oil until thick. On a serving plate, place a generous helping of pesto sauce, and top with two lamb chops per portion. *Serves 3-4.*

SEA SKRAUT

BJ, the dean of New York doorman and I often discuss **travel and food**. He has given this recipe to a number of our guests. We are not sure of the origin of the name or its spelling, but we are sure of its taste.

2 lbs of smoked pork butt (brisket of beef or duck legs may be substituted)
3 lbs curly cabbage
4 medium potatoes, peeled and cut into ½ inch slices
1 small clove garlic
2 tbsp. paprika
1/8 cup vegetable oil
3/4 cup flour
Water

Place the meat in a large pot and fill with water until half the meat is covered and cook for 1 hour under medium heat. Remove the meat from the pot and set aside.

Cut the cabbage into quarters, and place in the same pot with the cooking liquid. Cook cabbage about 40 minutes until soft. Place the sliced potatoes in the cooking pot 20 minutes after the cabbage. Remove the pot from the heat and set aside.

In a large skillet heat the oil and brown the garlic, slowly add the flour stirring continuously, be ready to add the cooking liquid to the flour mixture, in small amounts, as the flour begins to bubble and dry. Continue to add the cooking liquid and stir until all the flour has reached a smooth consistency. Add the flour mixture to the cabbage and potatoes (be sure to pour off excess cooking liquid, so only about 1 cup remains). Next, add the paprika and mix everything thoroughly. .

Slice the meat about ½ inch thick and place on a large plate. Place the cabbage and potatoes on the side of the meat. Garnish with sweet and sour pickles and hot mustard. *Serves 6.*

JACK AND SUE'S BAKED BEANS WITH SAUSAGE

The only way to get through a **Nor'easter** on Nantucket

DeMarco
RESTAURANT

4 28oz. cans baked beans (good quality-drain liquid)
2 lbs. linguica (Portuguese sausage)
1 lb chourico (Portuguese sausage)
1 cup pure maple syrup
1 cup ketchup
1 large red onion, chopped

Thinly slice linguica. Halve each section of chourico, then remove the casing; halve each section again, then thinly slice. (Note: meat slices more easily if partially frozen.) Place sliced meat and chopped onion in a slow-cooker set on low. After an hour, add drained beans, maple syrup and ketchup. Stir gently but thoroughly. Set cooker on high for an hour or two, or until liquid appears bubbly. Reset cooker on low until ready to serve.

Crusty bread and hearty red wine are good accompaniments. *Serves 15 to 20.*

VEAL CHOP WITH ALMONDS AND THYME

This dish becomes more **popular** every year.

1/2 cup of breadcrumbs
2 tbsp. dry almonds, finely chopped
1 tbsp. thyme
2 tbsp. finely chopped bell peppers
1 tbsp. garlic
4 tbsp. olive oil
2 medium veal chops (approximately
8-10 ounces).
Preheat oven to 350 degrees.

In a bowl, whisk together all the breadcrumbs, almonds, thyme, bell peppers, garlic and 2 tablespoons olive oil. Rub as much of the mixture as possible on both sides of the veal chop. Reserve the remaining mixture and set aside.

Let the veal sit for 10 minutes. In a skillet, heat the remaining 2 tablespoons of olive oil. With a spatula, carefully lift the coated veal chop onto a hot pan and sear one side for about 2-3 minutes. While it is cooking, press the remaining herbs into the uncooked side that is facing up. Turn the chop over carefully and sauté for 3 minutes, then place in a 350-degree oven for 6-8 minutes. *Serves 2.*

ROAST CHICKEN AND FRESH HERBS

Amazingly simple, this many-flavored roast chicken has a **"home, sweet home"** quality about it. Served with potatoes and a green salad, it makes a wonderful dinner.

For the chicken:
1 large roasting chicken 4-5 lbs
1 tbsp. paprika
1 tbsp. sea salt
1 tsp. black peppercorns
1 tsp. fennel seeds
1/4 cup cornmeal

1 bunch fresh thyme
1 bunch fresh mint
1 bunch fresh parsley
1 whole lemon

For the sauce:
Leaves of fresh herbs (above)
Sea salt
Coarsely ground black pepper
1/4 cup fruity olive oil
1/4 cup fresh orange juice
1/2 cup white raisins, chopped

Remove the innards from the chicken and discard (or save for soup.) Wash and pat dry the chicken. Rub the paprika, sea salt, black peppercorn, fennel seeds and cornmeal thoroughly inside the cavity.

Wash the fresh thyme, mint and parsley, keeping them in bunches, shake off the excess water. Cut off about 1 inch from the very ends of the stem. Stuff fresh herbs and half a lemon (cut into 6 slices) inside the cavity, packed tightly. Place the other half of the lemon over the cavity to create a seal.

Rub the outside of the entire chicken with paprika, sea salt, black peppercorn, fennel seeds and cornmeal. To ensure the seasoning adheres, rub the surface with a bit of honey. Bake in a 450-degree oven for 45 minutes.

When the chicken is done and the liquid runs clear, place on a serving board. Remove the lemons and bunched herbs. Discard the lemons. Remove stems from the herbs and place leaves in a food processor. Blend to a compact consistency. Add the sea salt, coarse black pepper, olive oil, fresh orange juice, and the chopped white raisins. Place the entire mixture in a sauce pan, bring to a boil and simmer for 5 minutes. With a sharp carving knife, quarter the chicken.

Paint the bottom of a serving plate with the heated sauce; place one of the quartered chicken pieces in the center. Add more sauce as desired. Serve remaining sauce in a bowl. *Serves 4.*

Jeffrey Allen

THE STOCK POT

DeMarco
RESTAURANT

Veal Stock:

25 veal bones (8 -10 lb)

10 yellow onions

8 carrots

1 bunch celery

4 whole bay leaves

1 bunch thyme

4 tbsp. black pepper corns

4 qts. red wine

In a 20 quart stock pot, cover with cold water

Preheat oven to 450 degrees.

Most people shudder at the very thought of making stock from scratch, thinking it an elaborate, difficult undertaking. Not only is a homemade stock far better tasting than any of the commercial canned products found in grocery stores or supermarkets. Like all good things, it does take time, but worth every minute

The most difficult part is resisting its delicious aroma while you wait. The stock can be frozen until you make your next soup or a recipe that calls for water. It adds superb flavor to a rice or pasta recipes. Better yet, it is a far less fattening (and better tasting) alternative to cooking oils. Pair down the following recipe to the amount you can use. All basic stocks are made essentially in the same manner, with slight variations in the main ingredients. Fish stock is cooked for one hour.

Roast the veal bones in a 450 degree oven for about 45 minutes. Coarsely chop the onions, carrots and celery. Add them to the pot with the herbs and peppercorns. Put the roasted bones on top. Reduce the red wine by half and add it to the stock pot. Now cover the ingredients with cold water and simmer for 8 hours. Strain the liquid. Utilize for cooking immediately or reserve and freeze for future use.

If you want to reduce it further to make a demi-glace, pour the stock back in a pot, lower the heat and reduce by half.

THE NEW MEAT LOAF

This is one dish that has to be on everybody's **"Top 10"** comfort food list. While we do not serve it in the restaurant, we include it here because this recipe is particularly tasty, as well as very healthy. Scalloped potatoes make a perfect accompaniment for this loaf.

DeMarco
RESTAURANT

The ingredients:
1 pound of very lean ground beef
1 pound of very lean ground turkey
1 cup of instant oatmeal
½ cup of bread crumbs, ¼ inch size
1 cup of fresh spinach cleaned, thoroughly drained and chopped (frozen spinach may be substituted).
½ cup of tomato ketchup
2 eggs, beaten
½ cup of diced cheddar cheese
¾ cup of whole pistachio nuts
2 cloves of garlic, finely chopped
1/3 cup of scallions and stems, finely chopped
1 tbsp. of rosemary, finely minced
1 tbsp. nutmeg
Sea salt and black pepper to taste

For the "sauce":
¼ cup tomato paste
¼ cup ketchup
1 tbsp. white wine vinegar
1 tbsp. honey

In a large bowl, place the ground beef and ground turkey, oatmeal, bread crumbs, spinach, ketchup, eggs, cheese and nuts. Mix thoroughly but do not pack. Let stand for 30 minutes.

In a skillet, add olive oil, scallions, garlic, rosemary, nutmeg, sea salt, black pepper, and sauté for 6-8 min, until soft. Cool for 15 min, and then fold into the meat mixture.

Place the entire mixture in a large loaf pan and pat down lightly and evenly. With a knife, make a 2-inch deep cut along the entire length of the meatloaf. Spread the cut apart with a fork on each side, so that it opens like a crevice.

In a separate bowl, whisk together the tomato paste, ketchup, white wine vinegar and the honey. Mix thoroughly and fill in the cut along the entire meatloaf. Bake in a 375-degree oven for 45 minutes. *Serves 8-10.*

ONE-POT SUPPER

The following recipe can produce a dinner for **50 people**. The key to cooking for a crowd without sacrificing quality is to use the appropriate techniques to that end. This recipe is quick and simple.

For the stock:

2 tbsp cooking oil (preferably olive oil)
3 whole cloves of garlic, peeled
1 large Vidalia onion, thinly sliced (not diced)
4 medium carrots cut into ¼-inch pieces
4 stalks of celery, cut into ¼-inch pieces
1 medium bell pepper, cut into ¼-inch pieces
1/4 cup parsley (flat or curly)
1 tbsp. dry mustard
Sprig of rosemary
1 tsp. black peppercorns
2 qts. of low-fat, low-sodium chicken stock

For the meat and vegetables:

2 lbs. of lean, cubed white turkey breast
1 lb. double-ground turkey*
3 lbs. lean beef, cubed
1 lb. lean double-ground beef*
2 lbs. potatoes (preferably Russet or Yukon Gold), scrubbed, unpeeled, eyes removed, cut into ½- inch dice
1 lb of white cannellini or navy beans (if canned, drain)
4 lbs. hard, European-style veal, beef or poultry, such as Italian, Spanish or German sausage (preferably cooked), sliced
Into 1-inch pieces
1 lb frozen peas
1 lb whole cherry tomatoes
1/2 cup good sherry

For the garnish:
Sour cream
Fresh mint sprigs

One-pot suppers are simple, nutritious, and delicious; they are an ideal way to feed a lot of people very efficiently, and often very economically as well. From hearty soups, stews and casseroles, everything in one pot with the proper seasoning lends itself to culinary delight, good taste, good nutrition, since no nutrients are wasted in the cooling liquids. (An Italian comedian was once quoted as saying, "We never knew what we would have for supper, but we knew it would be served with a ladle.") This dish is a great way to grasp the concept of an easy method of cooking for a crowd In the summer, when fresh vegetables are plentiful, or even in winter frozen substitutions will do, a great one- pot supper can always be enjoyed.

The following recipe can produce a dinner for 50 people. The key to cooking for a crowd without sacrificing quality is to use the appropriate techniques to that end. This recipe is quick and simple; it could be made even more elegant by the addition of tiny meatballs instead of plain ground meat. Accompanied by a hearty Spanish or Italian red wine, a large slice of crusty country bread and a simple salad of beefsteak tomatoes and red onions, the one-pot dish is transformed into a soul-satisfying meal.

In a large pot, heat the oil. Add the garlic, onions, carrots, celery, bell pepper, parsley, dry mustard, peppercorns and rosemary. Cook for five minutes over medium heat until soft or translucent (not browned). Add the cubed beef and chicken stocks; simmer for 2-3 minutes. Add the cubed turkey; simmer for another 2-3 minutes. Bring to a slow boil. Add the ground turkey, ground beef and potatoes. Simmer for 20 minutes. Add the beans, sausage, frozen peas, cherry tomatoes and the sherry. Simmer for another 35 minutes.

Serve in a large bowl with a dollop of sour cream and garnish with fresh mint. *Serves 40-50.*

*Note: Ask your butcher to double-grind the meat, which will produce an interesting texture in the final dish.

UMIDO DI PESCE OR BOUILLABAISSE

This dish was featured in the **New York Times**, front page of the Living Section, February 15, 1984, as an example of health and good taste.

1 teaspoon minced garlic
2 tablespoons olive oil
1 tablespoon chopped fresh basil or 1 teaspoon dried
½ pound swordfish, cut into 1-inch pieces
½ pound salmon, cut into 1-inch pieces
2 tablespoons extra virgin olive oil
2 1½-pound lobsters, split and quartered
1 tablespoon minced garlic
1 tablespoon tomato paste
1 cup dry white wine
6 to 8 cups "muddy" fish broth (see recipe)
1 tablespoon saffron threads
2 dozen mussels, scrubbed
1 pound medium shrimp, peeled and deveined
1 pound bay scallops
8 slices crusty Italian bread, toasted and rubbed with garlic
clove and drizzled with extra virgin olive oil
4 tablespoons rouille (see recipe)
4 tablespoons chopped fine Italian parsley.

"Muddy" Fish Broth
5 pounds flat fish bones, cleaned and rinsed in cold water
1 head celery, chopped
1 bulb fennel, with stalks, chopped
1 large onion, chopped
1 bunch leeks, chopped
1 bottle dry white wine
2 tablespoons fennel seeds
1 ½ cups tomato paste
Pinch thyme
Pinch crushed black pepper.

Rouille
1 pinch saffron threads
1 pinch hot pepper flakes
6 tablespoons extra virgin olive oil
½ teaspoon minced garlic
1½ teaspoons lemon juice
1½ teaspoons tomato paste
1 egg yolk.

Soak saffron and pepper flakes in oil.

The article begins with "picture a steaming tureen of tender, plump seafood and firm, delicate fish in a savory broth of white wine, saffron and tomatoes. Inhale the aromas as the tureen is set down before you, the scent of saffron mingling with the fragrance of the impeccably fresh fish.

Mix the minced garlic, olive oil and chopped fresh basil and marinate the swordfish and salmon in the mixture for two hours.

Heat extra virgin oil in a heavy-bottom 4-quart pot until oil is very hot (when it ripples).

Add lobster, reduce heat and sauté until shells become bright red. Add garlic and tomato paste; stir and add wine. Cook over high heat until wine evaporates.

Add fish broth, saffron and mussels. Cover tightly, lower heat. When first mussel opens, after 1½ to 2 minutes, stir in marinated fish, shrimp and scallops. Cover, cook 1½ to 2 minutes; remove from heat.

Divide among four large warmed glass or earthenware soup plates or bowl. Top each with two slices of bread, each slice topped with 1½ teaspoons rouille. Garnish with chopped parsley. Serve immediately.

Yield: 4 servings

"Muddy" Fish Broth

Put the fish bones, celery, fennel, onion and leeks in a stockpot and cover with water. Bring to boil and simmer, uncovered, for about 40 minutes. Remove fish bones and leave remaining ingredients.

Add wine, fennel seeds, tomato paste, thyme and black pepper and cook over high heat until broth assumes the consistency of muddy water, thick and bubbly, 35 to 40 minutes.

Strain through fine mesh strainer. Cool.

Rouille

In stainless steel bowl, using a whisk, blend garlic, lemon juice and egg yolk and puree. Beat well and while beating, slowly add oil mixture to form a mayonnaise. Beat until all oil is incorporated. Taste and adjust seasonings. Chill.

Yield: Half a cup, more than needed for the fish stew.

FISH FILETS WITH CANNELLINI BEANS

This recipe leaves room for **substitutions**. Starting with your favorite firm white-fleshed fish, tuna or salmon, this dish is prepared with fruit juice and served with cannellini beans. The result is a colorful and multitextured meal.

For the fish:
Butter or substitute
4 (6-oz.) firm, white-fleshed fish filets, approximately 1-inch thick
8 tbsp. orange juice
4 tsp. lime juice.

For the vegetables:
1 cup cannellini beans

For the garnish:
mint leaves, finely chopped
basil leaves, finely chopped
orange zests
½ cup cherry tomatoes, halved

In a frying pan, sauté the filets in butter, orange and lime juices, until just cooked through. Sprinkle with mint and basil. Place the cannellini and the cherry tomatoes around the fish filets. Garnish with the mint, basil and zests. *Serves 4.*

FILET OF FISH WITH GREEN TOMATOES IN MOCK CREAM SAUCE

This dish tastes **seductively creamy**, but has absolutely no "bad" fats. The creamless sauce is just as good on pasta as it is on fish. As for the fish, any firm, white-fleshed fish or salmon will do well here.

For the mock cream sauce:
2 large green tomatoes (reserve 4 raw slices, thinly sliced)
Olive oil
1 tbsp. shallots, finely chopped
1 tbsp. garlic, minced
1 large white onion, chopped
1 green pepper, finely chopped
2 ripe Hass avocados, chopped into small pieces

For the fish:
4 (8-oz.) firm, white-fleshed fish or salmon fillets
Sea salt and pepper to taste

Cut one of the green tomatoes into 4 thin slices; set aside. In a little olive oil, sauté the shallots, garlic and onions. Add finely chopped green pepper and sauté until soft. Chop the remaining green tomatoes and add to mixture. Cook for 2 minutes. Transfer the mixture to a food processor, along with the avocados, and blend until smooth, slowly adding a few tablespoons of olive oil until it is slightly thicker than heavy cream (add a little water if it becomes too thick). Set aside. Sauté the whitefish filets in a little olive oil, 3 minutes to a side. Season with salt and pepper. Place mock cream sauce in a serving platter, then top with the 4 raw green tomato slices. Place fish filets on each of the raw green tomato slices. *Serves 4.*

STEAMED PRINCE EDWARD ISLAND MUSSELS

These marvelous, plump mussels' clean, briny taste reflect the **pristine sea** from whence they came. There is no fresher or tastier shell fish than those that come from the ocean of Nantucket.

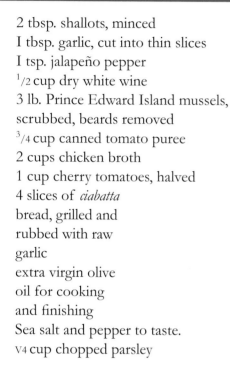

2 tbsp. shallots, minced

I tbsp. garlic, cut into thin slices

I tsp. jalapeño pepper

¹/₂ cup dry white wine

3 lb. Prince Edward Island mussels, scrubbed, beards removed

³/₄ cup canned tomato puree

2 cups chicken broth

1 cup cherry tomatoes, halved

4 slices of *ciabatta* bread, grilled and rubbed with raw garlic

extra virgin olive oil for cooking and finishing

Sea salt and pepper to taste.

¼ cup chopped parsley

In a hot sauté pan, sweat shallots, garlic and hot pepper for 1 minute. Add mussels and white wine; cook for 1 minute. Add tomato puree, stock and halved cherry tomatoes. Over high heat, cover and cook until mussels are just open, 2-3 minutes. To serve, place a piece of grilled garlic bread in a serving bowl; spoon the mussels and their liquid over the bread. Drizzle dish with olive oil and parsley. *Serves 6.*

BRAISED SHRIMP WITH CITRUS VINAIGRETTE AND PARBOILED VEGETABLES

This is a dish that **combines** the best of two worlds: fresh shrimp and aromatic vegetables.

The vegetables:

2 cucumbers

2 parsnips

1 yellow squash

1 lb. shrimp

For the marinade/vinaigrette:

1/2 cup white vinegar

1/2 cup olive oil

1/2 cup orange juice

1/4 tsp. cayenne pepper

1 tbsp. honey

Sea salt and pepper to taste

Cut vegetables into long strips about 1/4 inch thick. In a medium-size baking dish, place vegetable strips and shrimp in one layer on the bottom. In a large bowl, combine ingredients for the marinade/ vinaigrette and whisk until well blended. Pour 3/4 of the marinade over vegetables and shrimp. Refrigerate for at least one hour. Remove the marinated vegetables and shrimp, and braise for 5-6 minutes in the remaining marinade plus a little water to cover half of the ingredients in the pan. To serve, place the strips of vegetables parallel to each other, six to a plate, spaced 1 inch apart. Then place shrimp, three to a row, in spaces between vegetables. Drizzle remainder of the vinaigrette over the dish. *Serves 4.*

Ann Rich

WARM CHOCOLATE MOLTEN CAKE

This dessert was so popular that customers would call in advance to ask that a portion be reserved for them. When served, the chocolate inside the cake flows like lava.

½ stick butter
8 oz. bittersweet chocolate
4 whole eggs plus 4 yolks
½ cup sugar
6 tsp. all-purpose flour

In a double boiler, melt butter and chocolate; let cool. In another double boiler, combine eggs, yolks and sugar and gently cook until the mixture has doubled in volume. Fold the egg mixture into the cooled chocolate/butter mixture 1/3 at a time; sift in ½ of the flour. Repeat. Refrigerate for at least 3 hours or overnight. Bake at 375 F degrees for 12 to 15 minutes. *Serves 8.*

CAPPUCINO CHEESECAKE

Here is how to have your cake and eat it too, along with a wonderful coffee taste.

For the cake:
6 whole eggs
1 ½ cups sugar
2 tsp. vanilla extract
3 pounds cream cheese
1 tbsp. instant espresso
1 tsp. lemon juice
Pinch of salt

For the crumb coating:
4 cups bread crumbs
1 ½ cups sugar
½ pound melted butter
1 tsp. cinnamon

For the coffee mascarpone topping:
½ pound mascarpone
¼ cup powdered sugar
1 tbsp. coffee liqueur
1/8 tsp. salt
Sweetened whipped cream
Semisweet Chocolate shavings for garnish

Preheat oven to 325 F.

Combine all the crumb coating ingredients together and press onto the bottom of a 10-inch baking pan.

Not in a food processor, but a hand mixer, mix all the cake ingredients together on medium speed, until very smooth, without any lumps. Spoon the cream cheese mixture over the crumbs and bake for 3 hours. The Cheesecake must be baked in a water bath. *Serves 10.*

For the mascarpone topping, just mix (with a hand mixer) all the ingredients, do not over mix, spread on Cheesecake when the cheesecake is completely cool.

Garnish with whipped cream and the semisweet chocolate shavings.

Jeffrey Allen

TIRAMISU

Few desserts are as closely associated with **Italian cuisine** as tiramisu, with the possible exception of cannoli. This particular recipe is a classic for perhaps the most popular among them.

For the espresso syrup:
2 ½ cups sugar
2 tbsp. water
6 tbsp. espresso coffee
2 tbsp. coffee liqueur

For the filling:
3 egg yolks
¼ cup. sugar
2 tbsp. rum
1 cup mascarpone, softened
1 cup whipped cream
2 sheets gelatine, bloom

For the presentation:
3 dozen lady fingers
1 cup whipped cream, sweetened
1 tbsp. cinnamon
1 tbsp. cocoa powder
1 tsp. powdered sugar

In a double boiler, gently cook eggs and sugar until thickened. Add rum, and with a hand mixer beat on low speed until cool. Fold mascarpone and whipped cream into the beaten egg mixture. Soak lady fingers in the coffee syrup. Arrange them in layers, alternating them with the filling. Spread top layer with sweetened whipped cream. Combine cinnamon, cocoa powder and sugar; sprinkle over the whipped cream. *Serves 8*

Jeffrey Allen

CENTRAL PARK APPLE PIE

This year, I did gather enough to make three pies, which I transported to Nantucket and were prepared by our pastry chef.

For the crust:
5 tablespoons very cold milk
½ cup vegetable oil
2 cups flour
Dash of salt

For the filling
3 ½ lbs of Granny Smith Apples peeled, cored, and sliced
2/3 cup sugar
2 ½ tablespoons flour
3 tablespoons ground cinnamon
3 tablespoons melted butter

Preheat oven to 375 degrees.

Several apple trees grow in Central Park behind the Metropolitan Museum of Art. For years, I wanted to harvest those apples. I would pass by those apple trees almost every day and had often tasted them. They have a unique red vein throughout the white flesh. This year, I did gather enough to make three pies, which I transported to Nantucket and were prepared by our pastry chef. The pies were served at my table to my friends in Nantucket. They were impressed not only with the background story, but also with the spectacular taste of these rare apples.

For the crust, mix oil and milk together. Add flour and mix until mixture is moist. Do not handle dough too much, or it will become tough. Sprinkle some flour on a large piece of wax paper. Put the dough on the wax paper and sprinkle some more flour on top of the dough. Place another sheet of wax paper on top; Roll out dough between two sheets of wax paper. Place the dough into a medium-size pie pan. Cut the dough to fit the edges and save the extra crust. Refrigerate while you prepare the filling.

For the filling, in a large bowl, combine mix all of the remaining ingredients. Let sit for about 15 minutes. Transfer the filling onto pie crust.

Roll out the remaining dough and cut into 1 ½ inch strips. Weave the strips on top of the filling. Bake for 30-40 minutes, or until golden brown. *Serves 6.*

View from Central Park, behind the
Metropolitan Museum of Art.

REFRIGERATED CARAMEL ORANGE CHEESECAKE

This is a **wonderful** cooling end to a meal on a hot summer day.

For the crust:
1 ¾ cup graham cracker crumbs
2 ½ tsp. sugar
6 tbsp. butter, melted

For the filling:
1 ½ sheets gelatin, bloomed
1 ½ cups cream
½ cup cream cheese
½ cup sour cream
6 tbsp. sugar
½ tsp. vanilla extract
¼ tsp. vanilla bean

For the garnish:
Orange wedges (without the peel)
Sugar
Grand Marnier (optional)

Preheat oven to 350 F.

This recipe is for a 10 inch spring mold or individual 3 inch spring mold. The mold should be greased to avoid sticking. Combine all the crust ingredients. Bake for 4 minutes.

Bloom gelatin in ¼ cup cream. In a saucepan, heat ½ cup cream with the cream cheese, whisking until smooth. Add gelatine.

Whip together the remaining ¾ cup cream with sour cream, sugar and vanilla extract. Fold in the cream cheese mixture and fill mold(s). Allow to set overnight refrigerated. Unmold and garnish with orange wedges that have been caramelized by coating them in sugar water melted over low heat until syrupy and golden brown in color. Add Grand Marnier to melted sugar and orange wedges.

FRUIT CRISPS & CRISP TOPPING

This is the **quintessential** topping for any "crisp" worth its brown sugar.

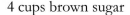

4 cups brown sugar
3 1/2 cups all-purpose flour
4 cup oats (1/2 quick, 1/2 regular)
1 tbsp. cinnamon
2 tbsp. salt
1 lb. butter, softened

3/4 cup canola oil

Preheat oven to 325 degrees.

Very popular among American dessert devotees, right up there with Mom's apple pie, the following "crisps" are variations on the same theme, where the basic changes are simply different selections of fruit incorporated in the recipe. The topping below can be used, unchanged, for all of them.

Combine all the crisp toppings ingredients. Rub in the butter and add the oil gradually until everything is combined to make a smooth paste to top the fruit. This crisp topping is suitable for all kinds of fruit fillings.

When ready, bake at 325 for 25 minutes. *Serves about 18.*

APPLE RHUBARB CRISP

When apples and rhubarb are a **marriage** made in heaven, which perhaps explains why the taste is near celestial.

De Marco
R E S T A U R A N T

2 lb. rhubarb
1/4 cup sugar
1/4 tsp. salt
1/4 cup sugar
2 lb. apples, peeled, cored and sliced
1/2 cup sugar
1 tbsp. lemon juice
1 tsp. vanilla extract
Pinch of salt
Macerate for 30 minutes, then add:
1/4 cup sugar, to make this mixture sweet enough.

Preheat oven to 325 degrees.

In a bowl, combine the rhubarb, sugar and salt; mix well. Let stand 30 minutes to draw out excess moisture. In a separate bowl, combine another ¾ cup sugar, apples, lemon juice, vanilla extract, and a pinch of salt. Macerate for 30 minutes. In a greased hotel pan, place the rhubarb and apple mixtures in alternating layers. Cover with crisp topping (above). Bake for 25 minutes, or until bubbling. *Serves about 18.*

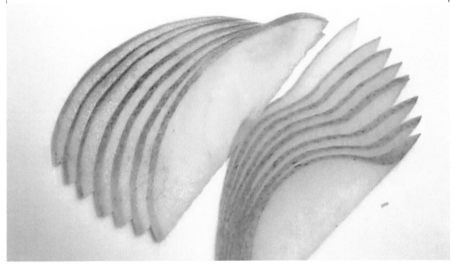

BLACKBERRY CRISP

Nantucket boasts of beautiful, jumbo-sized **blackberries** in season, a fruit less familiar perhaps than strawberries and blueberries, but just as delicious, with a unique flavor.

De Marco
R E S T A U R A N T

6 pints or 3 lb. blackberries
1 1/2 cups brown sugar
1 tbsp. vanilla extract
1 tsp. lemon juice
1/4 tsp. salt
2/3 cup tapioca (uncooked)

Preheat oven to 325 degrees.

In a large bowl, combine all the ingredients and macerate for 30 minutes. Arrange in hotel pan, top with crisp topping and bake for 25 minutes, or until bubbling. *Serves 8*

STRAWBERRY BASIL SORBET

On a hot **summer day**, there is probably nothing more refreshing than a sorbet. The two recipes below combine the traditional ingredient of fruit with the added, unexpected surprising taste of complementary herbs.

4 lbs. strawberries, puréed
6 tbsp. lemon juice
1/2 tsp. salt
1 1/2 cups corn syrup
1 1/2 cups sugar syrup
1/2 cup basil chiffonade

Mix all the above ingredients and pour in an ice cream maker. Churn until smooth. Transfer into a covered container; fold in the basil. Put in the freezer for about 3 hours or until set. *Yield 2 quarts*

LEMON THYME GRANITA SORBET

Come August, **iced desserts** are a real treat on sizzling afternoons.

1/4 tsp. fresh thyme, not minced
¼ tsp. lemon zest
4 cups water
2 cups sugar
1/2 cup + 4 tbsp. lemon juice
Pinch of salt

To infuse water, put water in saucepan in low heat, add the thyme, lemon zest and sugar. Cook for about 20 minutes, let cool, and pour through a fine strainer. Add lemon juice and salt, mix well.

Transfer to a stainless steel container, put in the freezer for about 4 hours or until set, stirring every 30-45 minutes to form ice crystals. *Yield 1 ½ quarters*

DeMarco
RESTAURANT

Don
DeMarco